THE TARNISHED GOLDEN YEARS*

A Guide to Parenting Your Elderly Parent

WENDY L. HARRISON

www.assistyoursenior.com

*Yes, I know that gold doesn't tarnish but
please allow some poetic license!

ISBN: 1-4904-4300-2
ISBN-13: 978-1-4904-4300-3
Library of Congress Control Number: 2013911450
CreateSpace Independent Publishing Platform
North Charleston, SC

DEDICATION

This work is dedicated to all my inspirational clients who have educated me on wisdom, patience, dignity, and how to run the marathon of life. I may not have learned all the lessons well—yet—but that is entirely my fault.

ACKNOWLEDGEMENTS

First and foremost, I am grateful to my husband, Bruce, who kept telling me throughout my years of working with seniors, "you should write that down." Now, I have! Besides being my biggest supporter, I am thankful for his suggestions during this endeavor and help in the editing of the manuscript.

I am very much appreciative of those who provided encouragement and contributed to the process: Peggy Reich, who at ninety-five years young is an inspiration to us all; Cindy Gonzales, who gave me the "push" I needed; and Cheryl Ross, who shared the travails of being a newly minted senior.

And a very special thanks to my mother, Mary. Through numerous examples, she taught me the value of caring for our elders. I know she's in heaven baking pies for the other angels!

BE ADVISED!

The information contained in this book is not a substitute for seeking advice and counsel from professional healthcare workers, financial advisors, government agencies, attorneys, and others who are familiar with the individual requirements of your senior. As policies and regulations continue to change in all aspects related to senior care and living, the reader is encouraged to seek current information as appropriate.

TABLE OF CONTENTS

INTRODUCTION

I n 1960, French crooner Maurice Chevalier opined that "Old age isn't so bad when you consider the alternative." At that time, the average life expectancy in the United States was sixty-five. In 2010, it was almost seventy-nine. The typical citizen now has fourteen more years to adjust to declining physical and mental health while wading through increasingly complex and intimidating medical bills. Maybe Maurice had it wrong (just kidding).

The median age of my client base is eighty-five, and according to the Administration on Aging, longevity is definitely on the rise. As of 2009, persons sixty-five or older numbered 39.6 million, which was 12 percent of the U.S. population. By 2030, it is estimated that this number will grow to 72.1 million, just as Social Security benefits are projected to start drying up.

Somehow, someone led us to believe that our "golden years" would be carefree and much simpler. Nothing could be further from the truth. Due to longer life spans, the aging population faces a myriad of health and financial issues (for example, higher rates of dementia and the depletion of retirement savings that were once thought to be sufficient). Ongoing modifications in social welfare benefits are becoming more complex and confusing. By necessity, family dynamics have changed with children becoming the "parents" and parents becoming the "children." The adult child caretaker can certainly expect that his or her life will become more complicated as well.

In our youth-oriented culture, many people are not well informed about the aging process (test your knowledge of senior issues by answering the "Are You Senior Savvy?" questionnaire in the Appendix). Adult children are often hesitant and embarrassed to talk with their parents about the needs or problems their parents are experiencing—and often don't even know where to begin. Their parents also may be embarrassed or baffled about the changes that are taking place in their lives and do not want to burden their children. All parties could be in denial. When problems become so severe that immediate action is required, the family is left scrambling for solutions—often leading to hasty and ill-informed decisions.

This book provides a concise overview of the major issues and problems confronting the aging population and offers guidance in solving those problems. I wrote this book not only to assist the adult children of elderly parents but also those who are currently seniors or hope to become seniors someday. With more than fifteen years helping over one hundred clients and their families, I am writing from the trenches, not from the mountain top.

Bottom line: don't get depressed; get prepared!

CHAPTER 1

HOME SWEET HOME: HOUSING ALTERNATIVES

"I don't know how you feel about old age…
but in my case I didn't even see it coming.
It hit me from the rear." —Phyllis Diller

———————————————

One of the most challenging issues facing an aging person is deciding where to live once mobility, health, or dementia problems arise. In most cases, this decision has to be made by a family member as the senior may have already lost his or her ability to provide input to the process. If the wrong choice is made, family relationships and financial security could be impacted for years—or forever.

There are a variety of accommodations that are available for senior citizens. You will need to assess your parent's mental, physical, and emotional condition to determine which type of housing suits his or her needs, including staying in his or her home. If you require help with this assessment, seek counsel from geriatric case managers, doctors, social workers, and local social services. Agencies that assist families in determining the types of housing available in a certain area and facilitate fitting the senior with those housing options can be found by contacting county social services, local senior centers and on-line.

If at all possible, your parent's residence should be near at least one family member or legal representative. Occasions will arise when a decision maker's presence is required, sometimes on short notice. Close proximity will save on travel expenses, time, and long-distance phone charges. Of course, your parent's financial situation, and perhaps *yours,* will be a major factor in determining the choice of housing. With all this in mind, let's review the living arrangements that are currently available for seniors.

LIVING WITH AN ADULT CHILD

If you believe you are doing your parent a favor by offering them a place in your home, plan this major event carefully. Here are some questions to ask:

1. Why am I doing this?

2. Will I need to make renovations to my home?

3. Is my parent willing to make this move?

4. How will other household members react?

5. Is this a temporary or permanent move?

Why am I doing this?
You may be experiencing a sense of obligation, guilt, or altruism. None of these reasons will benefit you or your parent in the long run. In most cases, your effort will not be appreciated. If this happens, you may become angry that this grand gesture is not shown the gratitude you expected. Tempers will flare, feelings will be hurt, and, perhaps, irreparable damage may be done to the parent/child relationship.

If you think you can save on caregiving costs, you probably will be able to do so if you or another responsible family member (*not* a teenage son or daughter) will be available to provide caregiving services. However, what will the *true* cost be to you, your parent, and the rest of the family?

The other members of your household may not welcome the intrusion of grandma or grandpa into their daily lives. Schedules will, by necessity, change. Family members will be called upon to become caregivers or, at the least, "babysitters." The dynamics and interactions between parents, children, and grandparents will be altered, and not necessarily for the better.

Caregiving is often strenuous and emotional. Depending on the degree of your parent's dementia and/or physical impairments, you may be required to do some or all of the following tasks: set up medications, bathe, change diapers, heavy lifting (moving an immobile parent), prepare meals, and monitor activities. This is on top of scheduling doctor visits, transporting your parent to appointments, acting as a liaison with government and insurance agencies, reconciling medical expenses with insurance payments, and paying bills. You may have to do with less vacation time and, if you decide to take some time off, a respite caregiver will need to be interviewed and employed. Yes, it's a full-time job!

To be blunt, we are a selfish generation and our children are even more so. Patience and understanding are indeed virtues but most of us don't have enough stored in the virtue bank to deal with our hectic lifestyles and the daily monitoring of our parents. Making decisions based on what the neighbors, Aunt Jane, or your siblings will think could create disastrous results. You *can* be a good person by addressing the needs of your parent (such as ensuring that he or she is living in a safe envi-

ronment, has necessary medical care, and is carefully monitored), but you do not have to become part of the problem.

However, if you or a family member do decide to become
the main caregiver for your parent, you would be wise to seek
out free or reasonably priced resources that can help you deal
with the emotional, financial, and physical toll this job will
take. Check with your local social service agencies and senior
centers for resources, or visit:

- Administration for Community Living at
  www.acl.gov or call 202-619-0724

- Family Caregiver Alliance/National Center on
  Caregiving at www.caregiver.org, or call 800-445-
  8106 (the website provides resources by state)

If your parent cannot live unassisted but has savings or, better
yet, long-term care insurance, hiring a caregiver or moving
your parent into an assisted living facility is a better way to
unload a good portion of the day-to-day responsibilities.

At this time, it is important to point out that purchasing
long-term care insurance is one of the most prudent financial decisions that can be made to protect your parent's assets
and alleviate the financial burden on you, your siblings, other
relatives, and, if applicable, the government (see chapter
titled "Medicare & More"). It may be too late to enroll your
parent in a long-term care insurance plan because premiums
increase with age and health issues. Also, approval for a plan
is more difficult to receive if the applicant is advanced in age
and has certain medical conditions. However, it may not be
too late for you! Financial advisors, estate planners, social
service agencies, your state government and insurance com-

panies can provide you with information and assistance on the various types of policies that are available.

Will I need to make renovations to my home if Mom or Dad moves in with me?

Yes. Depending on the degree of your parent's dementia or physical impairments, remodeling of certain living areas will almost certainly be necessary. These renovations could be very small (securing handholds in the shower, in the tub, or by the toilet) or very large (adding an extra room to the house).

If any major work is required, *please* do not move your parent into your home until the work is completed! Hammering and riveting noises are not only annoying for an older person but are also very disconcerting and may cause further confusion. Mom or Dad can easily trip over extension cords, uneven flooring, and loose boards. If that happens, you will have a whole different set of problems!

And what about your bank account? Can you handle the construction costs? If adding a room or making a major renovation will create a financial burden, do not consider it. You may come to despise your parent and be angry with yourself for adding to your money woes (and your spouse won't be happy, either).

Case Study: One of my clients, age eighty-six, moved in with her son after her husband passed away. The son began renovating his home from top to bottom. Flooring was uneven—if there was any. Electrical cords for lamps, appliances, and carpentry tools ran every which way. The only exit from the house was through the front door to the porch and down a *plank* to the driveway! The renovation work continued for two years up to the day my client died. It was unfortunate that her remaining years were spent not only adjusting to the death of her husband and her medical ailments but also coping with an untenable living arrangement.

Will Mom or Dad want to move in with me?

Most likely, your parent will want to remain in his or her home. Even though grandpa or grandma adores the grandchildren, he or she probably will not want them underfoot day in and day out. Or, your parent may not be able to tolerate the thought that you will be "in charge," with the inevitable role reversal that occurs between an elder parent and an adult child. Becoming your roommate may be seen by Mom or Dad as another step toward loss of independence.

If you think that temporarily moving your parent into your home would be a good bridge to a more permanent housing solution, you are fooling yourself. First of all, it will take a lot of effort and money to keep moving Mom or Dad from one location to the next. Second, the more moves a senior parent makes, the more disoriented he or she can become. Third, what is seen as a temporary solution quite often becomes permanent. That's just the way these things go, no matter how determined you are to make a temporary arrangement remain temporary.

If it's financially feasible, keep your parent in his or her own home with caregiving assistance, since relocating your parent to a new environment may cause anxiety and confusion. Initially, your parent may balk at having a "stranger" in the home; however, providing caregiving help on an incremental basis may get him or her accustomed to the idea. You can compassionately but firmly explain to your parent that a move to a facility will be required to ensure his or her physical safety if in-home assistance is refused.

Now that I have, hopefully, presented a good argument against you becoming a caretaker in your home, let's review alternative housing and care arrangements.

SENIOR APARTMENTS

For some, this is a logical transition from living in and maintaining a home. No yard work and no home maintenance costs appeal greatly to an older person. This type of arrangement usually offers meals in a communal dining room setting, various social activities, and housekeeping services. If a senior has already disposed of his or her car, the apartment complex generally provides transportation service to doctor appointments and shopping. However, this service is limited to certain days of the week and times of the day, so either you or a hired driver may be required to get Mom or Dad to an appointment.

Senior apartments do not provide any kind of medical assistance and are not assisted living facilities. If there is a need for some form of support, you or your parent will be responsible for finding and paying separately for a caregiver.

Security is usually provided. Most apartment complexes are gated and visitors must sign in and out. However, residents have been known to pilfer from other residents, so you should ensure that your senior's apartment door is locked at all times. If your parent's neighbor is suffering from dementia, remember that people so afflicted may wander in and out of apartments that are not secured.

BOARD AND CARE FACILITIES

Also known as residential care homes, these are ideal for those seniors who need assistance but prefer a more intimate setting. Also, the cost of a board and care facility is usually less than that of an assisted living facility. Board and care accommodations are mostly single-family homes in which bedrooms are rented out to seniors who have physical or mental health issues. Many find that the environment is less intimidating than a large assisted living facility. Depending on how much the senior or the family can afford, rooms may be shared. Due to the small size of the home, the residents are monitored more closely than in large assisted living communities. Meals are served, medications distributed, bathing assistance is provided, and residents are monitored. Social activities tend to be limited. Staff may be available to transport residents to appointments. Residents are free to roam within the house and within a fenced-in yard, but doorways that lead to the street are secured.

These homes are licensed and inspected by state agencies. In some states, it may be the Department of Health or the Department of Social Services. To determine which agency has this responsibility in your state, ask to see the latest inspection report (also known as a survey report). This report should be posted in the facility where residents and visitors can review it.

ASSISTED LIVING FACILITIES

The fees for rent and care at these facilities can be around five thousand dollars a month or more, depending upon the locality and the type of care your senior requires. Each resident pays a base rental fee for his or her apartment plus costs for "assistance."

Assisted living facilities offer safety, security, and twenty-four-hour support and access to care. A good facility should develop a personalized plan that meets the resident's needs and accommodates the resident's disabilities. Independence is encouraged, with most apartments offering scaled-down kitchens for meal preparation and parking spaces for residents' vehicles. Some facilities provide sections within the building just for people with Alzheimer's disease, where security and monitoring are much more stringent. Assisted living facilities usually offer many social events, communal dining, assistance with bathing, medication distribution, meals, laundry, and housekeeping, as well as transportation to appointments and shopping areas. Transportation varies by time of day and day of the week so a family member or hired driver could be required if the transportation schedule is not convenient.

"Assistance" may not be as readily available as you would like. Some residents hire caregivers, in addition to the facility staff, to help them with their needs. Though staff members monitor each resident throughout the day, they can be so rushed in administering to emergency situations or just dealing with a large volume of residents that they will overlook problems, or not report them. Do not expect your parent to receive the one-on-one attention that he or she would get if living with a caregiver at home.

Each state has its own licensing requirements for assisted living facilities. Visit the Agency for Healthcare Research Quality at www.ahrq.gov for information on your state's regulating agency.

CONTINUING CARE COMMUNITIES

Also known as "life care communities," these types of properties provide a continuum of care—from apartments and homes to assisted living and, if needed, skilled nursing care—all in one location. For many seniors, there is a great advantage to living in this kind of environment: they do not need to move from one place to another if their mental or physical functions deteriorate.

Here's the downside: continuing care communities are the most expensive of all long-term care options. They generally require a hefty entrance fee as well as significant monthly charges. Entrance fees can range from a hundred thousand to a million dollars. These fees are used to prepay for care as well as to provide the facility money to operate. Monthly charges can range from three thousand to five thousand dollars but may increase as the needs of the resident change. These fees depend on a variety of factors, including the health of the occupant, the type of housing he or she chooses, whether he or she is renting or buying, the number of residents living in the facility, and the type of service contract (see below). Additional rates may be incurred for other options including housekeeping, meal service, transportation, and social activities.

There are three basic types of contracts for continuing care communities:

1. *Life care or extended contract*—This is the most expensive option but offers unlimited assisted living, medical treatment, and skilled nursing care without additional charges.

2. *Modified contract*—This contract offers only some healthcare services for a set length of time and for a set fee. If the resident requires more services, the fees increase according to the market rate and the resident is financially responsible for those extra costs.

3. *Fee for service contract*—With this contract, the initial enrollment fee may be lower, but assisted living and skilled nursing will then be charged at market rates.

Be sure to ask: (a) if a contract can be broken, and if so, under what conditions, and (b) if the contract can be broken, what, if any, refund policy is available.

Be diligent in determining if the facility is financially sound and able to maintain its quality and service, and if it will be financially viable over the long term. Hiring an attorney to review the contract and an accountant to examine and evaluate the facility's finances would be worthwhile. Contact your secretary of state or your state's attorney general's office for information on continuing care communities.

In conclusion, the best housing option for your parent is to remain in his or her home, with caregiving assistance as needed. If Mom or Dad is amenable to downsizing and selling the family home, a senior apartment may be an appropriate choice. When physical and mental health issues prevent living at home or in a senior apartment, even with the help of a caregiver, you can research board and care facilities, assisted living facilities, or continuing care communities. Only as a last resort should you move your parent into your home. Wherever your parent ends up living, it is ultimately the family's responsibility to oversee the living conditions and evaluate the support that is being provided.

CHAPTER 2

"I'VE FALLEN AND I CAN'T GET UP"

"Don't let aging get you down. It's too hard to get back up." —attributed to John Wagner

———————————

Many of us probably remember the hokey television commercial portraying an elderly woman who has fallen and is lying on the floor, unable to get up under her own power. It advertised an alert system that the fallen senior activated to call for assistance. The commercial became a joke among those of us who were young and agile.

Now, our parents and possibly even we are at the stage in our lives when falling can have serious consequences. In 2010, according to the Centers for Disease Control and Prevention (CDC), 2.3 million older adults were treated in emergency rooms for non-fatal fall injuries, and over 662,000 of these patients were hospitalized. In people age sixty-five or older, falls are the leading cause of death by injury. The number of reported falls and death rates from falls has risen sharply over the past decade.

A study by Yale University researchers found that a person's health, rather than household hazards, is more of a factor in how frequently he or she falls and sustains injury. With age can come poor vision and hearing, weak leg muscles, confusion or dementia, a decrease in coordination, cardiovascular and neurological issues, and side effects from medications, which could impact a person's balance.

HOW FALLS CAN BE PREVENTED

To decrease the chances of falling from physical afflictions and to minimize the effects of a fall, seniors who are at risk should:

- schedule a physical on a yearly basis;

- have vision and hearing tested regularly;

- have a doctor or pharmacist review both prescription and over-the counter medicines to reduce side effects and interactions;

- exercise routinely and use weight training to strengthen leg muscles;

- wear rubber-soled and low-heeled shoes that fully support the feet;

- use a multi-footed cane or a walker for stability;

- position a walker or cane by the bed, chair or couch;

- purchase a portable potty chair to place next to the bed (many falls occur at night when the senior awakens to use the bathroom);

- get up slowly after resting or eating as low blood pressure may cause dizziness at these times;

- purchase couches/chairs that are at a proper height to allow the senior to get in and out of them easily (medical equipment and furniture stores sell chairs with mechanisms that "raise" a person out of a seating position);

- eat calcium-rich foods and take calcium supplements;

- limit alcohol consumption (even a small amount may affect balance);

- purchase an alert system, usually in the form of a pendant or wristband, to summon assistance in the event of a fall (some are waterproof and can be worn in the bath or shower).

To reduce hazards in the home that may contribute to a fall:

- ensure pathways are well lit and free of clutter;

- remove throw rugs and ensure other carpets are firmly attached;

- position grab bars both in and out of tubs and showers and near toilets;

- place nonskid mats and carpets on surfaces that may get wet;

- plug in nightlights or ensure light switches, as well as a telephone, are within reach of the bed;

- remove electrical cords and other wiring from walking areas;

- arrange furniture so it does not interfere with walking.

Many people with mobility problems do not use a walker or cane because they are more concerned with how they look and what others will think than with the consequences of a fall. They may also be in denial about their limitations. This is understandable but foolish. Men are more likely than women to die from a fall, but rates of fall-related fractures among older adults are more than twice as high for women.

In 2010, according to the CDC, the direct medical cost of falls was thirty billion dollars. As the elderly population increases, it is estimated that this cost will rise significantly. "I've fallen and I can't get up" isn't a joke anymore, is it?

MEDICAL EQUIPMENT/FURNITURE FOR MOBILITY ISSUES

Unfortunately, many of my clients have taken spills (usually trying to get out of bed at night) and have severely hurt themselves. They have required hospitalization, surgery, casts, or many months of wound care services. As one ages, bone loss and circulation problems compound the ability for the body to heal quickly or properly.

The purchase of an alert/monitoring device can reduce the negative effects of many falls. However, your senior must ensure that it is worn, and not left on the bedside table or on the kitchen counter. The initial installation cost for the device is reasonable, as is the monthly fee. Even if your senior is residing in an assisted living facility, such a device may be necessary. Residents are not closely watched all hours of the day and, when they do fall, may not be able to reach the inter-com/alert system that is installed in their room by the facility.

Please see the chapter titled "Medical Equipment and Devices" to review products designed to help those people with mobility problems.

CHAPTER 3

SELECTING A CAREGIVER — WHO WILL WATCH THE WATCHERS?

"Growing old is like being increasingly penalized for a crime you have not committed." —Anthony Powell

---

Finally! You have found a caregiver for your mom to ensure that she takes her medications, bathes regularly, and eats properly, as well as to generally watch over her; but who's watching the caregiver? Most likely, no one is.

When caregivers are not monitored (whether in the home or a facility), elder abuse may occur in the form of neglect, physical violence, emotional distress, or financial fraud. (See the chapter titled "Elder Abuse.")

If the family does not live nearby or does not have the time to devote to supervising the senior's living situation, geriatric care managers (or case managers) can be hired through agencies or privately. These case managers will assess how well the senior is functioning and will provide a care plan with specific recommendations to ensure that the senior receives the appropriate medical and/or psychological attention. They can secure services such as legal and financial guidance and can assist in finding home care, nursing care, or long-term care, in addition to counseling family members. See the chapters titled "Your Personal Support Group" and "Health Care Advocacy" to learn more about these professionals.

SELECTING A CAREGIVER OR CAREGIVING AGENCY

If you select a caregiver through an agency, ask for agency references and proof of liability insurance, and inquire as to how background checks are performed on caregivers. Find out if the agency provides case managers who will monitor the caregivers and the overall needs of the senior. A contract between the agency and the client, or the client's designee, should be signed before the agency performs any service. Check with your state or county (district attorney, state attorney general, county social services) to determine if the agency has received any complaints. For more information on caregiving, contact the Administration for Community Living at www.acl.gov or call 202-619-0724.

Caregiving agencies track caregiver hours and submit invoices that note the name of the caregiver, dates of service, and the hours worked. It is a good idea for you to also create a timesheet on which the caregiver can log his or her hours. Your timesheet can be used to reconcile the hours with the agency's invoice. See sample "Caregiver Timesheet" in the Appendix.

If you are considering using a caregiver who has come to you through an ad or referral from a friend, check all references thoroughly. Have the caregiver provide you with (1) a valid identification card, which notes a current address, (2) auto license plate number, and (3) his/her Social Security number. You should then perform a background check; there are a number of websites that offer background checks for a fee. As added protection, you may wish to require that the caregiver purchase a business services bond. A bond acts as insurance against any fraudulent or dishonest act that causes a loss. These bonds can be purchased in various amounts. You should be aware that the bonding company does not do background checks on the insured and will only cover the loss upon conviction of the insured.

When hiring an independent provider (who could also be a family member), a written contract should be made to protect both parties. The contract should include:

- a written job description (make a checklist of duties for the caregiver with the option of amending the checklist at a later time)

- a daily schedule that details the duties the caregiver needs to accomplish during work hours

- the name of the caregiver and the name of the employer (client)

- the rate of pay and the payment schedule

- the hours the caregiver is expected to work

- the expenses incurred by the caregiver that will be reimbursable

Two originals of the contract should be signed and dated by both the caregiver and the client, or the client's legal representative. One original is given to the caregiver; the other is given to the client to be filed in a safe place.

MONITORING THE CAREGIVING SITUATION

If employing an independent caregiver, create a timesheet that the caregiver can use to log his/her hours, mileage, and reimbursable expenses. (See an example of the "Caregiver Timesheet" in the Appendix.) Mileage is tracked when the caregiver uses his/her own vehicle to run errands for the client, such as shopping or driving the client to doctor appointments (ask to see a valid driver's license and proof of auto insurance if the caregiver is transporting your parent). The mileage rate can be paid at the allowed IRS rate or one that is mutually agreed upon. Pay the caregiver with a check, not cash, so that you have a record of payments.

A word of caution: Caregiving agencies are responsible for reporting the caregiver's income and for withholding/ paying Social Security and other taxes for that person. If your parent hires an independent caregiver, that person may be considered an employee by the IRS. Not only will his/her income need to be reported but also withholdings from that income must be made for state disability insurance and Social Security and Medicare taxes. Your parent may be required to file employment verification forms, certifying that the caregiver is legally entitled to work in the United States. Contact a tax or elder law attorney or a certified public accountant for information and advice.

Whether you employ a caregiver through an agency or one who works independently, you will need to set up a petty cash fund from which the caregiver can take money for groceries, medications, and so forth (keep no more than three hundred dollars in the cash account). Having a credit card on file at the pharmacy will eliminate the need for petty cash for medications. The caregiver should submit store receipts for all cash used. As a way of tracking expenses, see the sample "Petty Cash Account Log" in the Appendix. ***The caregiver should never have access to checkbooks or credit, debit, or ATM cards.*** Periodically review the petty cash fund, credit card statements, checkbook, and bank statements for any fraudulent use.

It is unethical (and a sure warning sign) for a caregiver to request a loan of money or other property, to request an advance in pay, or to ask the senior to make purchases for them. Remember, the senior is not a lending institution!

Make it a point to drop in unannounced to check on your parent and evaluate the caregiver. *This recommendation should be followed even if you are using a caregiver who has been hired through an agency.*

To reiterate, if you are unable to personally monitor your parent's caregiving arrangement, contact a geriatric care manager or case manager to do so. When the caregiver knows that someone is closely scrutinizing his/her activities and the welfare of the senior, abuse (financial or otherwise) is less likely to occur.

CHAPTER 4
ELDER ABUSE

"Growing old—it's not nice, but it's interesting." —August Strindberg

———————————————

In general, elder abuse falls into four categories:

- *Physical abuse* includes hitting, burning, restraining, or giving too much medication or the wrong medication. Though the incidence is low, it may also include sexual misconduct. (See chapter "Sex and the Senior Citizen.")

- *Emotional (psychological) abuse* involves shouting, swearing, threatening, or humiliating a person.

- *Financial abuse* consists of illegal or unauthorized use of a person's property, money, or other valuables. This would include changing a person's will to name the abuser as an heir or obtaining a power of attorney in order to swindle the person out of money or other property.

- *Neglect* includes depriving a person of food, heat, clothing, comfort, or essential medication.

According to the National Center on Elder Abuse, the Bureau of Justice Statistics reported that there were 5,961,568 cases of elder abuse in 2010. The median age of the victims was eighty. Much abuse goes unreported due to a feeling of shame on the part of the victim, the ability of con artists to "string victims along" until it's too late, or failure of family members to spot a problem and intervene.

As noted by the National Center on Elder Abuse in the above study, almost 60 percent of reported abuse is neglect. Much of this neglect is attributed to the fact that family members live far away from their elderly relatives. Gone are the days when the extended family resided just down the road or in a neighboring town. If a son or daughter has little contact with his or her parent other than making an occasional phone call, he or she often has no knowledge of the parent's living environment and deteriorating health. In some cases, adult children are estranged from the parent or there is no family remaining.

Therefore, it is critical that neighbors or anyone who has interaction with an elderly person be attuned to signs of neglect and that they report the situation to the local police department or to adult protective services. These outward signs may include disorientation, failure to follow simple instructions, inability to write out a check, or a disheveled appearance.

The senior's home is the most common setting for abuse. Perpetrators could include anyone in a position of control or authority such as a spouse, relative, neighbor, or caregiver. And don't forget people who prey on the elderly by devising scams on the Internet, through the mail, or by coming door-to-door.

Predators target many types of seniors: those who have no family or friends closely involved in their lives, those who live alone, and those who suffer from physical impairments such as blindness or hearing loss or who have a form of dementia. Also targeted are seniors who are just plain lonely. The need for companionship can make seniors vulnerable to a predator who might use this loneliness to take advantage of them.

In my work with seniors, financial abuse was the most prevalent form of abuse that I encountered. In one case, a caregiver embezzled twenty-five thousand dollars—all of which was found in cash under her bed! Another caregiver stole a cell phone and ran up two thousand dollars worth of charges. One asked for an advance in pay, received it, and then left town. A trusted granddaughter, who also had power of attorney over her grandmother's affairs, embezzled thousands of dollars out of her grandmother's bank account, opened several credit card accounts under the grandmother's name, and racked up fifty thousand dollars in credit card charges.

Unfortunately, in many cases, it is difficult to bring the perpetrator to justice. The reasons for this vary: the perpetrator may have fled the area, the victim's memory of the fraud is impaired, the victim may have "willingly" written checks or donated other valuables to the caregiver or family member, the victim has passed away before the case goes to trial, or the district attorney has "bigger fish to fry" and will not pursue prosecution (see chapter titled "Organization-The Key to Success" for information on combating financial fraud).

In order to protect your parent from financial scams, you must be aware of the people involved in his or her life and diligently check the backgrounds of outside services, agencies, contractors, and others who are hired to perform work inside or outside of the home. Regularly monitor credit card, bank, and other financial statements; track bills that are not being paid; be on the alert for notices of eviction or discontinued services. Review signatures on checks or other documents that look suspicious. Look for personal property, such as jewelry, that has gone missing (better yet, place valuables in a safe or safe deposit box).

You may not be able to monitor your parent's financial matters for a variety of reasons. If you are not confident in delegating the job to another family member, or if you suspect financial abuse by anyone inside or outside the family, you should hire a third party who can provide oversight. For referrals, contact a certified public accountant or local social services.

Certain individuals are legally mandated to report known or suspected instances of elder abuse. These include medical professionals, clergy, employees of healthcare facilities, and individuals who assume responsibility for the care or custody of an elderly person. Anyone who suspects that abuse has occurred should report it, either to the local police department or to adult protective services. Persons reporting abuse are shielded from both criminal and civil liability. An elder's assets, health or life may depend upon a call to the appropriate authorities. For more information, visit the website of the Administration for Community Living at www.acl.gov or call 202-619-0724.

CHAPTER 5
MEDICARE & MORE

*"If I'd known I was gonna live this long
[100 years], I'd have taken better care
of myself." —James Hubert Blake*

T he word "insurance" will possibly make you flip to a different chapter or run for cover. Most of us do not like to pay for insurance, nor do we understand how our insurance policies work. We often feel intimidated and, usually, will stuff insurance paperwork into a drawer to review at a much later date—if ever. Nevertheless, insurance is a necessary product or, as some would suggest, a necessary evil.

It is a very good idea to have at least a basic understanding of the types of insurance available for your elderly parent. It is also critical to familiarize yourself with your parent's current insurance plans before a crisis occurs. This will save you much time, energy, and grief when an occasion arises that requires your involvement in medical issues and finances. Remember, your parent's financial well-being is at stake!

Before you panic, please be aware that there are attorneys, agencies and social service groups (both private and governmental) that can assist in navigating you through the insurance maze. For personalized health insurance counseling and for help in making health coverage decisions, contact your state's health department at www.medicare.gov/contacts or call 1-800-633-4227. Additional resources are noted throughout this chapter.

As you may already know, the coverage offered by government insurance programs such as Medicaid and Medicare is constantly changing, as is that of private insurance carriers. To ensure that you receive the most up-to-date information available, contact the appropriate agencies before you make any decisions regarding your parent's insurance coverage.

An entire book could be (and has been) written just on the subject of government and private medical insurance programs for the elderly. However, the intent of this chapter is to provide concise and simplified information for the reader, or as simplified as I can make it considering that government bureaucracies are involved. Toward that end, I have created a synopsis of the various insurance programs.

MEDICAID

Each state operates a Medicaid program that provides health coverage for lower-income people. This group includes families with children, the elderly, and people with disabilities. Medicaid pays for healthcare services that meet its definition of "medically necessary," such as doctor visits, prescription drugs, hospitalization, x-ray and laboratory expenses, and nursing home care. Not all medical service providers accept Medicaid.

As of this writing, the Medicaid program is in flux, primarily due to the enactment of the "Patient Protection and

Affordable Care Act of 2010." It is advisable that you contact Medicaid by accessing www.medicaid.gov or by calling your state's Medicaid agency. You may also wish to consult with an elder law attorney who is an expert at maneuvering through the Medicaid bureaucracy. Check out the website for the National Academy of Elder Law Attorneys at www. naela.org to review their member directory, or call them at 703-942-5711.

MEDICARE

Individuals are eligible for Medicare if: (1) they are sixty-five or older and eligible for Social Security or Railroad Retirement Benefits, (2) they are sixty-five or older and their spouse is eligible for Social Security or Railroad Retirement Benefits, (3) they are under sixty-five and have been receiving Social Security disability benefits for at least twenty-four months, or (4) they are of any age and have permanent kidney failure requiring dialysis or a kidney transplant.

Participation in the Social Security program is the primary criteria for eligibility. If your parent or his or her spouse has not participated in the Social Security program or does not have the required credits to qualify for Medicare, he or she may purchase Medicare insurance. To find out the number of credits a person has earned, or for information on purchasing Medicare insurance, call the Social Security Administration at 800-772-1213, or visit www.ssa.gov.

Once a year, Medicare mails a handbook, "Medicare & You," to beneficiaries detailing medical services that are covered. This information can also be found on the Medicare website at www.medicare.gov or by calling 800-633-4227.

Currently, Medicare has four different parts:

1. *Medicare Part A* is hospital insurance and helps cover inpatient care in hospitals, skilled nursing facilities, hospice, and home health care. Part A will not cover all hospital costs and there is a deductible per benefit period. Part A coverage has already been paid through Social Security taxes.

2. *Medicare Part B* helps pay for doctor services, outpatient care, some preventative services, diagnostic tests, ambulance transport, durable medical equipment, and supplies. Part B generally pays 80 percent of the charges that are approved by Medicare and there is an annual deductible. Part B is optional and monthly premiums are deducted from Social Security benefits.

3. *Medicare Part C,* also known as the Medicare Advantage Plan, is similar to a Health Maintenance Organization (HMO) or a Preferred Provider Organization (PPO). You will need to use a healthcare provider within the network. These plans are administered by private insurance companies that have been approved by and are under contract with Medicare. The plans include Medicare Parts A and B and sometimes other coverage like prescription drugs, vision, and hearing. In addition to the Part B premium, a monthly premium for Part C is usually required.

4. *Medicare Part D* is an option that helps cover the costs of prescription drugs. It is run by private insurance companies that have been approved by and are under contract with Medicare. Enrollment

in Medicare is required, with the patient paying a monthly premium for Part D insurance.

You may have heard a lot of negative press about a "donut hole" associated with Medicare Part D (this is not an edible feature of the plan!). The term "donut hole" originally referred to a coverage gap in the insurance plan whereby, once the patient and the plan combined had spent $2,840 for covered drugs (including deductibles, copayments, and coinsurance), the patient had to pay the full cost of prescription drugs until the out-of-pocket expenses reached $4,550. Then, voila, the patient emerged from the "donut hole." If all this sounds like something a drug-addled mind would think up, just thank your members of Congress.

The "donut hole" rule has now changed. The coverage gap still exists but, while the patient is in that gap, he or she pays 47.5 percent of the plan's cost for covered brand-name drugs and 79 percent of the plan's cost for covered generic drugs. Once out of the "hole," the patient pays a small co-payment for covered drugs for the remainder of the year. By 2020, the "hole" will be closed completely. Until then, just watch where you step! For more information, see the chapter titled "The Elephant in the Room—Obamacare."

Note: Some medical service providers do not accept "assignment" from Medicare. In other words, they do not accept the Medicare-approved amount as payment in full. This means the patient may be charged more than the Medicare-approved amount - but there is a limit. The provider can only charge up to 15% over the Medicare-approved amount. This "limiting charge" only applies to certain services. If the healthcare provider does not accept assignment from Medicare, they must still submit a claim for services to Medicare on the patient's behalf. Due to the passage of the "Patient Protection and Affordable Care Act of 2010," it is anticipated that more service providers will not accept assignment from Medicare or will not accept Medicare patients at all.

A senior should enroll in Medicare Parts A, B (or C) and D three months before reaching the age of sixty-five, whether or not he or she is still working. If coverage is declined by the senior at the time of eligibility, late enrollment penalties and increases in premiums may apply.

If your parent has been receiving Social Security or Railroad Retirement Benefits (RRB) before age sixty-five, he or she will automatically be enrolled in Medicare Parts A and B. This is also the case if your parent is under age 65 and has been receiving disability benefits from Social Security or RRB for twenty-four months. (The beneficiary may decline Part B coverage.) Medicare will mail an insurance card to the beneficiary a few months before his or her eligibility date.

For enrollment questions, contact Social Security at 800-772-1213 or visit www.medicare.gov

MEDIGAP (SUPPLEMENTAL INSURANCE)

Medicare usually covers only 80 percent of Part B medical expenses. It also does not cover the full cost of Part A inpatient hospitalization. Supplemental policies offered by private insurance companies that are contracted with Medicare can be purchased to assist with paying out-of-pocket expenses, such as the costs that Medicare does not cover (copayments, coinsurance, and deductibles). Many of these Medigap insurance companies also offer prescription drug plans, known as

Medicare Part D. An individual enrolled in Medicare Part C cannot have a supplemental plan.

Supplemental insurance companies require that individuals have both Medicare Part A and Part B to be eligible to enroll in a plan. The best time to purchase a plan is during open enrollment. This period lasts for six months and begins on the first day of the month in which the insured is sixty-five or older and is enrolled in Medicare Part B. (Some states have additional open enrollment periods.) In most cases, after the initial enrollment period, the option to purchase supplemental insurance may be limited and may cost more.

For information on Medigap policies, call Medicare at 800-633-4227 or visit www.medicare.gov/medigap or call your state's insurance department.

Reimbursement from Medicare and Medigap/Supplemental Insurances

In most circumstances, the medical service provider first bills Medicare for medical charges incurred. After Medicare pays its portion of these costs, the remaining charges will be billed to the supplemental insurance. The patient will receive statements from Medicare and the supplemental insurance carrier that will reflect the name of the medical provider, date of service, amount billed, amount approved, and amount paid by insurance. Medicare only sends out statements, called Medicare Summary Notices, every three months unless Medicare is making a reimbursement payment to the patient.

If Medicare denies payment for a medical procedure or service, the supplemental insurance will not reimburse for that procedure or service. The patient can challenge Medicare's denial in writing (I have successfully done so on behalf of my clients). If Medicare reverses its denial and pays for the claim, the supplemental insurance will also do so. Information on how to file an appeal can be found in Medicare's handbook, "Medicare & You," and is noted on the Medicare Summary Notice.

It can be daunting when the deluge of paperwork from Medicare, the supplemental insurance provider, and the medical service provider comes rolling in. Many people just throw up their hands and assume that the charges have been processed correctly and that the final bill from the healthcare provider is accurate. That is not always the case.

When reviewing invoices from medical service providers, be sure that both Medicare and the supplemental insurance carrier have been billed and have paid their portion of the charges before final payment is made to the provider. It is wise to set up a system to track charges and payments. This system does not need to be complex, nor do you even need to create one on a computer. See the sample "Medical Billing Reconciliation Form" in the Appendix that can be used to ensure services have been billed and paid appropriately. By tracking bills and payments, you will be acting in a fiscally responsible way and will be helping to conserve the patient's financial resources.

VETERAN'S BENEFITS

If your senior has served in the military, he or she may be entitled to medical services, programs, and insurance through the Veterans Administration (VA). Some of the programs and services offered include disability benefits, healthcare, life insurance, long-term care benefits, dependents' and survivors' benefits, and burial benefits. For more information, visit the nearest VA office, call 1-800-827-1000, or access their website at www.va.gov.

TRICARE

This health insurance is available to both active and retired military personnel and their families. Plans are divided by regions of the country as follows: North Region (including the Eastern states), South Region, and West Region. Visit the website www.tricare.mil for contact phone numbers and information or call 866-307-9749 (North), 800-554-2397 (South), and 800-558-1746 (West).

LONG-TERM CARE INSURANCE

This type of insurance pays for all or a portion of the costs incurred when the beneficiary requires care for a long period of time in his or her home, in a skilled nursing facility, or in an assisted living facility. Long-term care insurance policies differ based upon the triggers that initiate payment, but most offer benefits based on either a beneficiary's severe cognitive impairment or the need for assistance with at least two or three daily living activities. These activities usually include bathing, dressing, eating, or using the bathroom.

Policies can be purchased with fixed daily benefits for a fixed period of time, such as three or five years, but are also offered for an indefinite period of time. Premiums vary widely depending on the policy holder's age at the time of purchase, the length and amount of coverage, and policy characteristics. These characteristics include whether benefits are adjusted for inflation and the length of any waiting period before benefits begin to be paid.

If your parent had the foresight to purchase long-term care insurance, you and your parent are indeed fortunate. Some people deem this type of insurance unnecessary and a waste of money. In over fifteen years of working with seniors, my experience has shown me that this is a critical insurance to have. Neither Medicare nor Medigap insurances cover extensive long-term care needs.

As most people are aware, we are living longer thanks to better knowledge about nutrition and exercise, plus medical advancements. If we are lucky, we will die in our sleep. However, statistics suggest that this is unlikely. According to the U.S. Department of Health and Human Services, 70 percent of the U.S. population will need long-term care at some point after the age of sixty-five, either at home or in a facility. Don't count on a child, other family member, or friend who will be willing to devote caregiving time to someone whose mental or physical condition is in decline.

In 2010, the median cost to live in an assisted living facility was $3,500 per month. Depending on the type of assistance needed and the area of the country, the cost could go as high as $8,000 (or more) a month. That works out to around $100,000 a year. In-home caregiving assistance averages about twenty-five dollars an hour. If your parent should require around-the-clock care, the service provider will usually charge a flat rate. Currently, this rate runs as high as $350 per day. In this case, the yearly cost is about $128,000. Unless you are extremely wealthy, these figures should give you pause—if not heartburn.

If your parent does not currently have long-term care insurance and he or she is in fairly good health, it would indeed be beneficial to research some plans. The older one gets and the more physical and mental problems one has, the more difficult and costly it is to purchase long-term care insurance.

Some experts believe that long-term care insurance should be considered if your assets are between $200,000 and $1.5 million and you wish to protect those assets for a spouse or heirs. Others argue that with the rising cost of healthcare and increasing longevity, even assets of three to five million may be drained in order to pay for long-term care. Another possibility to consider is that one spouse may need to live in a nursing facility but the other can remain at home. Then there must be enough money to cover two separate living expenses.

This type of insurance is probably not for you if (1) you can't afford the premiums for the necessary coverage; (2) you anticipate not having enough money to cover premium hikes that may occur during the time you own the policy; or (3) your net worth is less than two hundred thousand, as Medicaid will pick up the caregiving expenses after you exhaust your funds. You should consult with an elder law or estate attorney for more information regarding Medicaid requirements.

Government regulations are always changing regarding Medicaid, so it is best not to assume that the level of coverage Medicaid now provides will remain the same in the future. And, as a socially responsible citizen, you should financially prepare for your future medical needs (cut out the every-morning lattes) and leave Medicaid assistance to those who truly need it.

Long-term care plans are complicated, and offer many different options. Estate or elder law attorneys and *independent* financial advisors* are good contacts for information and for help in determining the needs of the policyholder.

Other resources that may be of assistance include:

1. the U.S. Department of Health and Human Services which provides some very useful information, such as the average cost of long-term care by state and in cities within that state; the department can be contacted at www.longtermcare.gov or by phone at 202-619-0724

2. the American Association for Long-Term Care Insurance at www.aaltci.org or 818-597-3227

3. the National Association of Insurance Commissioners at 866-470-6242

4. Medicare at 800-633-4227 or visit www.medicare.gov/ltcplanning

5. your state's insurance department (contact Medicare to get the phone number)

Before you choose a plan, be sure to check the insurance company's rating with your state's insurance department. You want to make certain the company is financially sound and will still be in business when the insurance is needed.

---

* An advisor who is employed by a brokerage firm, bank, or insurance company offers advice on products that are promoted by their financial institution. Their legal allegiance is to their employer and not to the client. An independent financial advisor offers objective advice on all financial products on the market and, by law, must represent the client's best interest. Independent advisors are Registered Investment Advisors (RIA) or Investment Advisor Representatives (IAR) who work for Registered Investment Advisors.

A couple of final notes: (1) All insurance companies will issue a card for the policyholder. Be aware of where your parent's cards are located as it will be easier for you when you need to interact with the insurance carrier. Also, medical insurance cards should be readily available since they will be required for admittance to hospitals and other medical facilities, and by doctors' offices for billing purposes. (2) Due to strict privacy laws, only the patient can discuss his or her health issues or benefits with a representative of any government agency, insurance company, or medical facility. Most likely, there will come a time when you will need to interact with Medicare, an insurance carrier or doctor's office on behalf of your parent. In order to avoid a lot of frustration, request an authorization form from the agency, company or doctor's office which will allow your parent to designate you as his or her representative. To discuss your senior's Medicare benefits, contact Medicare and request the "Authorization to Disclose Personal Health Information" form.

CHAPTER 6

THE ELEPHANT IN THE ROOM: OBAMACARE

"Old age ain't no place for sissies." —Bette Davis

Very few Americans (including the lawmakers who voted for it) have either read or understand the piece of legislation called the "Patient Protection and Affordable Care Act of 2010," or "Obamacare." And no wonder: its two statutes total a whopping 961 pages, while its current regulations exceed 20,000 pages.

THE "PATIENT PROTECTION AND AFFORDABLE CARE ACT OF 2010" AND ITS IMPACT ON THE AGING POPULATION

The law is intended to provide affordable healthcare for all Americans. It mandates that certain employers provide health insurance to their employees and that most citizens purchase health insurance, and it promises to lower medical costs and insurance premiums. Under the law, insurance companies will not be able to deny coverage for any reason, and young adults may remain on their parent's insurance plan up to age twenty-six.

Until the "Affordable Care Act" is fully implemented, analysts and pundits acknowledge that the public, politicians, and healthcare providers have no clear idea of the law's ramifications. Though the law was to be fully implemented in 2014, several of its mandates have been delayed; over one thousand businesses and unions have been granted or are seeking waivers from provisions of the law; and special consideration has been given to members of Congress and their staffs to assist them in paying for "Obamacare" coverage. In addition, some insurance companies are pulling out of certain markets and insurance premiums are continuing to increase, as are medical costs.

The uncertainty created by the ongoing changes to this legislation places another burden on your caretaking responsibilities. As the law progresses into the different stages of its implementation for Medicaid and Medicare recipients, it will be up to you to track its effects on your parent's healthcare.

The table below compares the government's stated opinion of the law's effects with those of various analysts.

Federal Government's Position	Analysts' Position
1. The patient's existing guaranteed Medicare-covered benefits will not be reduced or taken away. The patient will still have the ability to choose his or her own doctor.	1. According to the Congressional Budget Office (CBO), the law reduces Medicare reimbursements to hospitals, nursing homes, skilled nursing facilities and hospices by $716 billion over ten years. The National Center for Policy Analysis states that these cuts in payments will result in providers having to drop Medicare patients. Many seniors will need to find services provided by community health centers and safety net hospitals. They may not have the option of choosing their own doctor.

2. The life of the Medicare Trust Fund will be extended as a result of reducing waste, fraud, and abuse, and of slowing cost growth in Medicare, which will provide the patient with future cost savings on premiums and coinsurance. (*Writer's comment: (1) Medicare's Part A Trust Fund is projected to be insolvent by 2026. The total program has promised $35 trillion worth of benefits to current and future seniors that are not yet paid for; (2) Note the use of the term "future." Premium and coinsurance payments will rise, at least through 2017, according to the Medicare 2012 trustees report.)*	2. In its "Issue Brief" of November 1, 2012, The Heritage Foundation explains that the law mandates $716 billion in Medicare payment cuts over the next ten years but these cuts are not targeted at specific instances of waste, fraud, and abuse. The cuts represent changes in payments to healthcare providers. That money cannot simultaneously be used to pay for the new law and extend the life of the Medicare Trust Fund
3. If a patient has high prescription drug costs that put him/her in the "donut hole," he/she will receive a 50 percent discount on covered brand-name drugs while in that "donut hole." The "donut hole" will be closed completely by 2020.	3. This will save beneficiaries about $43 billion over ten years according to the Urban Institute. The CBO's 2010 estimate indicates that "enacting those changes would lead to an average increase in premiums for Part D beneficiaries of about four percent in 2011, rising to about nine percent in 2019."

One provision of "Obamacare" creates a panel of fifteen experts who will make up the Independent Payment Advisory Board. When the program's spending surpasses the budget target, this board will propose recommendations to lower Medicare spending. However, these are not just proposals since they become law automatically if the Secretary of Health and Human Services decides to implement them. Congress can take steps to deter implementation of the recommendations if it so chooses. There seems to be no doubt from analysts that this portion of the law will affect the type of services that seniors receive.

The Medicare 2012 trustees report states that, under Obamacare, the standard Medicare Part B monthly premium will rise between 2012 and 2017 from $99.90 to $128.20, while the Part B deductible will climb from $140 to $180. The hospital deductible for Medicare Part A will increase from $1,156 to $1,336, as will co-insurance costs. The law initially mandated a $156 billion reduction in payments to the Medicare Advantage program between 2013 and 2022. However, as reported in April 2013, the Centers for Medicare & Medicaid Services reversed that provision, announcing an increase in payments. If you are getting dizzy by all this back and forth, take some Dramamine. It will be cheaper than seeing a doctor!

Medicare payroll taxes will also increase on high-income earners (individuals with an annual income of $200,000 and couples with an annual income of $250,000) from 2.9 percent to 3.8 percent. The law also extends the 3.8 percent Medicare tax to investment income.

In recent budget proposals, premiums for Medicare Parts B and D would increase by 15 percent for upper income earners. However, 25 percent of all Medicare beneficiaries would see those increases by 2035. New fees would be imposed on the "baby boomers" who join Medicare in 2017. This proposal increases the Part B deductible by $25 for new beneficiaries in 2017, 2019, and 2021. Since a Federal budget has not been enacted for several years, it's anybody's guess if these proposals will be implemented or if new ones will be forthcoming.

Many of these rules and regulations will change over time. This makes it virtually impossible for you to build a plan for your parent's financial future without some guidance and assistance. Seek the help of an elder law attorney or an *independent* financial advisor to steer you through this morass. Most importantly, have a candid talk with your parent's physician and other healthcare providers to determine how the law will affect their practice and treatment of their patients.

CHAPTER 7
SOCIAL SECURITY

"We've put more effort into helping
folks reach old age than into helping
them enjoy it." —Frank A. Clark

When Social Security was created in 1935, the intent was to benefit only retired people. In 1939, the program was changed to add survivor's benefits and benefits for the retiree's spouse and children. In 1956, disability benefits were included.

Retirement benefits are calculated using the number of "credits" earned and the beneficiary's year of birth. Full retirement age was sixty-five for many years but the regulations were changed in 1983. For people born in 1938 or later, that age gradually increases until it reaches sixty-seven for those born after 1959. However, one can start receiving reduced benefits at age sixty-two if he or she has earned forty "credits." A person's full retirement age and benefit amount can be determined by accessing his or her Social Security Earnings Statement online at www.ssa.gov or by calling 800-772-1213.

In the most current report by the Social Security Administration, a shortfall of funds is estimated to occur by 2033. However, the Congressional Budget Office (CBO) indicates that the reserves may be exhausted before that date due to higher disability claims, low interest rates, and high unemployment (fewer employed workers means fewer taxes being collected for Social Security). When the reserves run out, incoming taxes will only be able to cover about 75 percent of the program's current promised benefits. How will that 75 percent be distributed? No one knows.

REGULATIONS REGARDING BENEFITS, MARRIAGE, AND DEATH

Though the future of Social Security remains uncertain, here are the current regulations that may pertain to your parent's situation:

- Even if a spouse has never worked under the Social Security program, that spouse may be able to receive benefits if he or she is at least sixty-two years of age and his or her spouse is eligible for retirement or disability benefits. He or she can also enroll in Medicare at age sixty-five.

- If a spouse is eligible for retirement benefits on his or her own work record, Social Security will pay that amount first. However, spouses are entitled to benefits of up to 50 percent of the higher earner's benefit if that amount is greater than the payments based on his or her work record. Got that?

- Upon the death of a spouse, Social Security will pay a death benefit to the surviving spouse of $255. As soon as it is possible, Social Security should be notified of the death of a beneficiary. If a monthly benefit payment has already been made to the deceased, Social Security will, depending on the date of death, require that the payment be returned.

- A widow or widower can receive reduced benefits as early as age sixty or full benefits at full retirement age. If the surviving spouse is disabled, benefits may be received as early as age fifty, depending on when the disability occurred.

- If a widow or widower remarries after he or she reaches age sixty (age fifty if disabled), the remarriage will not affect his or her eligibility for survivor's benefits.

- A divorced spouse is eligible for benefits based on his or her ex's allowance if the marriage lasted at least ten years. When the divorced spouse remarries, he or she generally cannot collect benefits unless that most current marriage ends.

- A surviving divorced spouse could receive the same benefits as a widow or widower provided that the marriage lasted ten years or more. Remarriage will not affect his or her eligibility for survivor's benefits if he or she remarries after the age of sixty, or age fifty if disabled.

- Recipients receive their Social Security benefits by direct deposit into a bank account or by paper check. To save taxpayers money, a new rule was established in March 2013 that discontinued paper checks. If the beneficiary does not have a bank account, his or her benefit payment is to be loaded onto a prepaid Direct Express Debit MasterCard. However, as of this writing, due to complaints by a consumer group, this rule will not be enforced—though it will be strongly recommended.

- In many instances, it is no longer necessary to make a trip to the Social Security office as online services are available for such things as applying for benefits, changing address or direct deposit information, and accessing earnings statements.

- Around each November or December, Social Security sends a notice advising what the next year's benefit payment will be, less any deductions such as Medicare premiums. For tax purposes, the beneficiary also receives a 1099 form in January that details the previous year's payments and deductions.

- Government rules and regulations are always changing. For more information and updates on the program, you may visit the Social Security website at www.ssa.gov, call your local Social Security office, or call 1-800-772-1213.

Ensure that you know your parent's Social Security number (if you have a copy of his or her Social Security card, that's even better) and how benefit payments are received. Due to privacy rules, Social Security representatives will not discuss questions you may have regarding your parent's benefits. However, your parent may complete the "Consent for Release of Information" form to designate you or another responsible party as a contact person. This form can be obtained from the Social Security website or by calling the agency.

Besides Social Security benefits, your parent may also be receiving payments from a pension plan or annuity. In some cases, he or she may just receive a pension and no Social Security. Take time to review all retirement and annuity benefits that your parent is receiving.

CHAPTER 8

LOSS OF INDEPENDENCE— TAKING AWAY THE CAR KEYS

"Regular naps prevent old age, especially if you take them while driving." —Unknown

---

The aging population suffers from various debilitating physical and mental conditions that can lead to frustration, depression, and feelings of uselessness. In short, the elderly feel they no longer have control of their lives.

Coping with loss of independence may be one of the most traumatic experiences your parent will face as he or she ages (it is right up there with death of a spouse, child, or dear friend). Since adult children usually have not yet experienced this type of loss, many tend to make light of the issue and do not take it seriously. That is a mistake.

PHYSICAL AND MENTAL CONDITIONS THAT LEAD TO A LOSS OF INDEPENDENCE

Physical and mental losses include difficulty in walking, climbing stairs, getting in and out of the bath, deteriorating vision and hearing, less energy, memory problems, and the onset of dementia. In many cases, the physical and mental problems combine to create a drastically different lifestyle and one that relies heavily on outside assistance and influence.

HOW SENIORS REACT TO LIFESTYLE CHANGES

People vary in their reactions to their restricted lifestyle. Some are quite willing to hand over the car keys and receive help from others; most are not. Their reactions are complicated. Overwhelmed and frustrated with their new vulnerability, many seniors become fearful and resentful. They do not want to become dependent on family and friends, but at the same time they expect those family and friends to always be available for them. Others feel guilty because they believe they are becoming a burden to their relatives. Most will long for the past and for how things "used to be." The senior will likely fret over the increase in expenses due to services and assistance which he or she is resentful in needing.

Mom or Dad will require assurance that losing independence is common as people age and is not a sign of personal failure; it's normal to feel sad and frustrated. Your parent may need help from a doctor, mental health professional or social worker to acknowledge deteriorating health issues and to understand how those issues affect not only his or her life but also the lives of others. For example, your parent's insistence on driving, even with physical and mental conditions that limit his or her driving ability, increases the likelihood of injury to others. This irresponsible behavior also risks your parent's life savings in the event of a lawsuit.

Many elderly people believe it is their duty to leave an inheritance for their children. Consequently, they resist spending money in their "golden years" for the support and care that is necessary. It is important for them to recognize that the financial sacrifices they made over the years were intended to pay for the care they require at this point in their lives. Encourage your parent to accept assistance from caregivers, drivers, and bill payers. If Mom or Dad has input in making hiring decisions, he or she might be more agreeable to accepting outside support.

It is essential that your parent retain as much of their independence as possible. To this end, work out the necessary arrangements for Mom or Dad to maintain relationships with family and friends, and offer encouragement for him or her to participate in relaxing and fun activities. Contact local social services about volunteer programs that provide companionship and outings for the housebound senior. After taking care of children, grandchildren, an ill spouse, or other relatives, it is now time for your parent to put his or her needs above others—in short, to become selfish.

However, regardless of the steps you take to improve your parent's quality of life, he or she may still become depressed. Clinical depression in the elderly is common and affects about six million Americans age sixty-five and older. It often occurs with lifestyle changes, illnesses, and disabilities. Even if the depression is mild, it can substantially increase the likelihood of cardiac and other diseases when not treated. Depression also increases the risk of suicide; the suicide rate of people between the ages of eighty and eighty-four is more than twice that of the general population.

Some common signs of depression include:

- loss of interest in hobbies, social activities, pastimes

- appetite or weight changes

- insomnia or oversleeping

- anger, irritability, agitation, or even violence

- loss of energy

- concentration problems

- reckless behavior such as substance abuse or compulsive gambling

There are several treatments available for elderly depression; these include medication, counseling or psychotherapy, and electroconvulsive therapy (ECT). Though most anti-depressants are effective, there are side effects that should be considered. Some anti-depressants can be sedating or can cause a sudden drop in blood pressure which can lead to lightheadedness and falling when a person stands up. They may take longer to start working in an older person. Psycho-therapy is beneficial for those who prefer not to take medi-cine and who have mild to moderate symptoms. Sometimes psychotherapy is recommended along with anti-depressant medications.

ECT can be used as a treatment for depression in the elderly when they are unable to take medications because of side effects or interactions with other drugs, or when depression is very severe. ECT is a procedure in which electric currents are passed through the brain, triggering a brief seizure that is thought to make changes in the brain chemistry. Though there has been a stigma attached to this treatment, it is much safer today because it uses electrical currents given in a controlled setting and is administered to people who are under general anesthesia.

County social service agencies, hospital social service departments, senior centers, church organizations, social workers, and healthcare providers can provide further guidance and information about dealing with the loss of independence and the resulting depression.

CHAPTER 9

IS IT DEMENTIA OR IS IT ALZHEIMER'S?

"Old age puts more wrinkles in our minds than on our faces." —Michel de Montaigne

———————————

There often is confusion among laypeople about various descriptions used to define mental deterioration. To clarify the terms used by the medical profession, *dementia* is an umbrella term for a group of cognitive disorders that are characterized by memory impairment. *Alzheimer's*, a progressive disease of the brain, is perhaps the most common form of dementia.

According to the Centers for Disease Control and Prevention (CDC), Alzheimer's usually occurs in people who are sixty years and older and is the sixth leading cause of death in the United States. The risk of a person developing it doubles every five years, starting at the age of sixty-five.

Some studies suggest that increased physical activity, good nutrition, maintaining social contacts, and participating in intellectually stimulating activities could lessen the risk of developing Alzheimer's. These studies also suggest that prevention of diseases that damage blood vessels (such as heart disease, strokes, and type 2 diabetes) plays an important role in minimizing the risk of contracting Alzheimer's.

The CDC states that current studies are investigating the use of vitamins C and E, as well as non-steroidal anti-inflammatory drugs for treatment of Alzheimer's. At this time, the studies have not determined the effectiveness of these treatments. However, there are approved medications for Alzheimer's that will lessen the symptoms and may slow the progression of the disease. There is no cure.

WARNING SIGNS

Some early signs of dementia include:

- a constant forgetfulness

- being unable to follow simple directions

- loss of interest in favorite pastimes

- putting things in the wrong places (milk carton in oven, purse in refrigerator)

- personality changes

A person suffering from Alzheimer's or other forms of dementia may have problems with planning, organizing, motor activity, and use of language plus difficulty in recognizing objects and people. In the early stages, a person will experience some memory loss. Eventually, a person's thinking ability decreases and he or she can no longer perform daily living activities.

DIFFERENT FORMS OF DEMENTIA AND ASSOCIATED CAUSES

Some other causes of dementia that produce symptoms similar to Alzheimer's include drug reactions, nutritional deficiencies, infections, brain tumors, poisoning, or a reduction (or cessation) of the brain's oxygen supply. In these cases, the condition may be reversible.

In addition to Alzheimer's disease, other diseases that present dementia symptoms include:

- Vascular dementia—this occurs as a result of brain damage from cardiovascular or cerebrovascular problems

- Lewy body dementia—protein deposits, called Lewy bodies, develop in nerve cells in regions of the brain involved in thinking, memory, and motor control

- Frontotemporal dementia—primarily affects the frontal and temporal lobes of the brain, which are associated with personality, behavior, and language; portions of these lobes atrophy; occurs at a younger age, usually between forty and seventy; often misdiagnosed as Alzheimer's or as a psychiatric problem

- Huntington's disease—causes degeneration in the brain and spinal cord and is hereditary

- Creutzfeldt-Jakob disease—believed to be caused by an abnormal form of the prion protein (normally, these proteins are harmless but, when they are misshapen, they become damaging)

With the onset of dementia, the afflicted person will most likely have some awareness of his or her declining mental faculties. He or she will become frustrated and fearful. It is critical that a physician be consulted as soon as possible for testing and a diagnosis. *Note: People suffering from dementia are very adept at "hiding" the onset of the disease and can present themselves as fully functional, especially if you do not have regular contact with them.*

It is imperative that you and others remain calm and patient when in the presence of your parent. In order to gain his or her trust for what will surely become a challenging road ahead, do not tell your parent "nothing is wrong" in a misguided attempt at reassurance. Your parent will know that's not true. It is not necessary to go into long, detailed explanations but whatever you tell him or her, make sure it's the truth.

A person may become more demanding and possibly violent as his or her memory loss and confusion progresses. Coping with this mental deterioration is a heart-wrenching experience for the family, and they may feel overwhelmed and powerless. If you find yourself in this position, here are some things to remember:

1. Accept the debilitating effects of this disease and the fact that your parent is no longer the same person who helped you with your homework. Do not push your parent into situations, socially or physically, that he or she cannot handle. Your parent may become agitated and, if the situation demands a lot of physical mobility, is more likely to fall.

2. Refrain from arguing with your parent. He or she no longer has the ability to reason. You

will only become frustrated and may provoke a violent reaction from your parent if you attempt to argue or correct him or her.

3. Do not expect your parent to follow instructions, even if written down. This is an exercise in futility. You or another caretaker will need to be responsible for ensuring follow-through on important items.

4. If you are on a guilt trip, cancel it. Your actions or inactions did not cause this disease. You have a responsibility to ensure your parent is in a safe environment, has medical attention, and is receiving appropriate caregiving. There is nothing more you can do.

For more information, insights, and assistance, contact your parent's physician, your county's social services, local hospital social service departments, or the following organizations:

- National Institute of Neurological Disorders and Stroke at www.ninds.nih.gov or 800-352-9424

- Alzheimer's Association at www.alz.org or 800-272-3900

- Alzheimer's Foundation of America at www.alzfdn.org or 866-232-8484

- Alzheimer's Disease Education and Referral Center of the National Institute on Aging at www.nia.nih.gov/alzheimers or 800-438-4380

CHAPTER 10

YOU ARE WHAT YOU EAT— SENIOR NUTRITION

"Everything slows down with age, except the time it takes cake and ice cream to reach your hips." —Attributed to John Wagner

---

For all of us, good nutrition keeps our bodies healthy, sharpens the mind, and energizes us for the long haul. Proper diet reduces the risk of heart disease, stroke, high blood pressure, type 2 diabetes, bone loss, cancer, and anemia. Unfortunately, many seniors develop poor nutrition habits due to a variety of circumstances such as:

1. living alone

2. onset of dementia

3. health issues (improperly fitting dentures, gum disease, intestinal problems)

4. diminishing senses of taste and smell

5. loss of eyesight

6. prescription medications

7. depression

STEPS FOR ENSURING
HEALTHY EATING

If your aging parent is living alone without any assistance, it is important that his or her eating habits are closely monitored. As unobtrusively as possible, open cupboards and the refrigerator to determine if there is adequate food in the house and that it consists of healthy choices. Offer to accompany your parent on grocery shopping trips so you can ensure he or she is buying nutritional food. Your parent will enjoy the company and appreciate the assistance.

It is important that your parent does not skip breakfast, lunch, or dinner. When your schedule allows, suggest helping your parent with the planning and preparation of a meal. This offer will not only delight him or her but will also ensure that your parent is eating properly. Ask friends or relatives to share meals, at their convenience, with Mom or Dad so that he or she is not always eating alone. *Note: Be on the lookout for chewing difficulties or loss of appetite, and seek medical attention immediately if these problems arise.*

If consistent healthy eating remains a problem, Meals on Wheels, a nonprofit volunteer program, offers meals delivered directly to the home. According to a survey conducted for the U.S. Administration on Aging, the Meals on Wheels program is highly rated by recipients:

- 85 percent say the program helps them eat healthier

- 87 percent say the program helps them improve their health

- 91 percent say the program makes them feel more secure

- 93 percent say that the program allows them to continue to live in their own home

- 91 percent rate the program's service as good to excellent

To find a nearby program, visit the website for the Meals on Wheels Association of America at www.mowaa.org or call your local senior center or social services.

Meals on Wheels is not a substitute for vigilant caretaking. Caregivers, social workers and family are responsible for ensuring that the senior is eating properly. "That's all well and good," you say, "but I'm not a nutritionist and I don't have time to research the subject." And that's why you are reading this book. Here are some guidelines, but you should also check with your parent's doctor.

HEALTHY NUTRITION HABITS

Calorie Intake

According to the National Institute of Aging, a woman over the age of fifty who is not physically active requires about 1600 calories a day; 1800 calories a day if somewhat active; 2000 calories a day if very active. A man over the age of fifty who is not physically active needs about 2000 calories a day; 2200–2400 calories a day if somewhat physically active; and 2400–2800 calories a day if very active. Balanced nutrition, however, is more than just counting calories.

Food Pyramid Groups

A diet that consists of fruit, vegetables, grains, protein, and calcium can contribute to a higher quality of life and more independence.

- Fruit: For more fiber and vitamins, two servings a day of whole fruits, rather than juices, are recommended (one medium piece of fresh fruit is equal to one serving; ½ cup of raw, canned, or frozen fruit is equal to one serving). Bananas and apples are great, but color-rich fruits like berries should also be added to the diet.

- Vegetables: Consuming about two cups every day of dark leafy greens (such as spinach, kale, and broccoli) and those veggies that are orange and yellow in color (such as carrots, squash, and yams) are the best choices.

- Grains: Seniors need six to seven ounces of grains each day with whole grains preferred over processed white flour.

- Protein: Sources for protein are fish, beans, peas, nuts, eggs, milk, cheese, and lean meats. Seniors need about .5 grams of protein per pound of body weight. You can calculate your senior's protein grams required by dividing the senior's body weight by two.

- Calcium: Adequate calcium intake can prevent osteoporosis and bone fractures. Milk, cheese, yogurt, broccoli, almonds, kale, and tofu are rich sources of calcium. Seniors require 1200 mg of calcium a day.

Essential Vitamins and Minerals

Because the body loses some of its ability to regulate fluid levels as it ages, seniors are prone to dehydration. Drinking water throughout the day and with meals can help to avoid constipation, urinary tract infections, and, possibly, confusion.

As we age, it is more difficult for our bodies to absorb vitamin B-12, which is found in meat, shellfish, cheese, and eggs. This vitamin is needed to create blood cells and maintain a healthy nervous system.

Vitamin D is critical to absorbing calcium and can be found in a few foods such as fatty fish, egg yolk, and fortified milk. We get most of our vitamin D through sun exposure but the skin is less efficient at synthesizing vitamin D when we get older.

Consult with your parent's physician for recommendations on vitamin supplements.

CHAPTER 11

USE IT OR LOSE IT – EXERCISE THE MIND AND BODY

"I still have a full deck; I just shuffle slower now." —Unknown

"They tell you that you'll lose your mind when you grow older. What they don't tell you is that you won't miss it very much." —Malcolm Cowley

---

LIVING A LONGER AND HAVING A MORE INDEPENDENT LIFESTYLE

Lo and behold, the "Fountain of Youth" has finally been discovered! It's called staying active—mentally and physically.

We know that physical exercise is important for everyone. A regular exercise program can prevent, or in some cases delay, certain diseases or conditions such as heart disease, diabetes, obesity, osteoporosis, and Alzheimer's. Exercise helps to reduce anxiety, depression, and arthritis pain; it increases mobility and provides for better sleep. Regular exercise can help older people stay independent longer.

However, muscle and joint pains start to become more pronounced as a person ages. Many seniors, some who were couch potatoes even before they made it to their "golden years," will say that they are just not up to exercising. This is no excuse, since a multitude of exercise regimens exist for older people.

There are several types of exercise that a senior needs:

1. Endurance activities such as walking, swimming, or riding a bike build "staying power" and improve the health of the heart and circulatory system.

2. Strength exercises build muscle tissue and reduce muscle loss.

3. Stretching exercises keep the body flexible and limber.

4. Balance exercises help reduce the chance of a fall.

5. Weight-bearing exercises keep bones healthy and prevent osteoporosis.

Consult with a doctor, physical or occupational therapist, personal trainer, or other licensed expert to determine the right program for your parent. Even a senior with mobility problems, who relies on a wheelchair or walker, can benefit from special exercise programs suited for his or her disability.

Your parent might be more agreeable to starting and continuing an exercise program if a family member or friend can join him or her once or twice a week. Also, some people do well and have more motivation when they are in a group setting. If your parent is motivated by joining a group activity, check with local agencies and organizations (such as a senior center) to find out about the programs in your area. Remember: while exercise is important, it needs to be coupled with good nutrition and other healthy habits.

Keeping the mind engaged with mental gymnastics, along with physical exercise and a healthy lifestyle, improves memory, sharpens the thinking process, and allows the senior to maintain control over his or her daily living. Some suggestions for mental exercise programs are:

1. Engaging in a new activity such as chess, a card game, painting, or pottery.

2. Starting a journal, or if computer savvy, a blog that provides a creative outlet.

3. Finding a subject that is of interest and researching it by using the Internet or the local library.

4. Searching the dictionary for definitions of words read or heard and writing a sentence or a paragraph using those words.

5. Playing board or computer games, puzzles, or group games such as bingo.

6. Breaking up a routine by doing different things each day.

7. Socializing with friends and family; avoiding becoming a recluse.

8. Reading—but ensure that the correct eyeglass prescription is used.

9. Organizing names of family members
    alphabetically, or by age, or by listing their
    names in order of their birthdays.

For more information and ideas on mental exercises,
contact your physician, local social services, or the Alzheimer's resource listing provided in the previous chapter.

CHAPTER 12

SEX AND THE
SENIOR CITIZEN

*"Age is a high price to pay for
maturity." —Tom Stoppard*

The topic of sexual intimacy may make children of elderly parents a bit squeamish. After all, if you find it difficult to discuss financial concerns, how on earth can you talk about sex with your eighty-year-old parent?

However, consider this scenario: You are skeptical about Mom's new boyfriend. Is he after the family fortune? Will Mom throw you and your siblings under the bus? You should be less concerned about what he may be taking from her and more concerned about what he might be *giving to* her.

SEXUALLY TRANSMITTED DISEASES

Change in the social culture, such as divorce and acceptance of out-of-wedlock sex, has facilitated more active sex lives. Sexually transmitted diseases (STDs) are not just for the young. They can be contracted at any stage in life and are often overlooked by seniors and their healthcare providers. Seniors are less likely to talk about their sex lives with their physicians, and since many physicians assume seniors do not have active sex lives, they may not ask.

There are numerous STDs that can complicate the lives of sexually active people of any age and can lead to other diseases if not promptly treated. Some of these diseases include genital herpes, gonorrhea, viral hepatitis, and syphilis. If paranoia is your thing and you desire a full-blown listing, visit the website for the Centers for Disease Control and Prevention (CDC) at www.cdc.gov or call 800-232-4636.

According to the CDC and the most current data available from 2005, persons age fifty and older account for nearly one quarter of all people with HIV/AIDS and 15 percent of new HIV/AIDS diagnoses. Twenty-five percent are living with HIV/AIDS, an increase of 17 percent from 2001. Symptoms of HIV/AIDS are often attributed to the aches and pains of normal aging, so the senior may be less likely to get tested.

The August 2007 *New England Journal of Medicine* cites a study concluding that many older adults *are* sexually active, with men being more so than women. Because education and prevention messages on the subject of STDs have not been geared to seniors, they very often know less than the younger population.

After having been in monogamous relationships for most of their adult lives, seniors may be unprepared for the "senior sexual revolution." Their sense of sexual security could change with a new sexual partner, particularly if the new partner has been around the block a few times. It may be up to an adult child to talk with Mom or Dad about the use of condoms and the wisdom of STD testing of potential sexual partners. Well, at least you won't have to explain birth control.

If your parent is embarrassed to be tested for STDs by his or her personal physician, blood-testing sites will perform confidential testing. These services can be found on the Internet or through your local county health department.

SEXUAL ABUSE

A darker side to the senior sexuality issue is sexual abuse. In 2010, of all the cases of elder abuse reported, .04 percent was attributed to sexual abuse. Though not significant, the number is very likely underreported, as is true in all categories of elder abuse.

Sexual abuse occurs more often in long-term care settings, such as assisted living facilities and nursing homes. A large percentage of residents in these facilities have some form of dementia and cannot convey the abuse to others or are too embarrassed to do so.

Sexual predators do not wear a sign on their foreheads announcing their intentions. They can be anyone in a position of power such as a doctor, nurse, caregiver, or family member who uses his or her authority to intimidate an elderly person. In a facility setting, even another resident is capable of sexual abuse.

The act of sexual abuse can include rape, unwanted kissing or fondling, any type of penetration, and exposure of body parts such as genitals or breasts. Even if a person is suffering from dementia, there are methods to determine if an assault has taken place (see below). Though physical signs may be covered up, emotional trauma is more difficult to hide.

Signs of abuse include:

Physical:

- bruises inside the thighs
- bruises on the genitals

- bleeding from the vagina or anus

- pain or itching in the genitals

- sexually transmitted disease

Mental:

- sudden change in behavior

- avoidance of physical and social contact

- a fearful, jumpy attitude

- depression

According to the National Institute of Justice (NIJ), sexual abuse is one of the most understudied aspects of elder mistreatment. An NIJ-sponsored elder sexual abuse study found that:

- Elderly sexual assault victims were not routinely evaluated to assess the psychological effects of an assault.

- The older the victim, the less likelihood that the offender would be convicted of sexual abuse.

- Perpetrators were more likely to be charged with a crime if victims exhibited signs of physical trauma.

- Victims in assisted living situations faced a lower likelihood than those living independently that charges would be brought and the assailant found guilty.

When sexual abuse is suspected, it must be confronted immediately by initiating an investigation, using the resources of adult protective services and law enforcement. If the abuse is being perpetrated by a resident or employee of a facility, inform the facility's management *and* local law enforcement. You may need to remove your parent from the facility on a temporary basis, or permanently if the problem is not resolved.

Whether your parent lives at home or in a facility, be cognizant of changes in his or her emotional and physical states. Carefully listen to your parent's complaints or concerns. If you are unsure as to what action to take, consult with adult protective services, healthcare professionals, and the local police department.

INAPPROPRIATE SEXUAL BEHAVIOR

Inappropriate sexual behavior occurs in about 15 percent of elderly people with dementia, being more common in men and in patients with severe dementia. This behavior can manifest itself in masturbation or disrobing in a public setting or improper touching of a caregiver.

It is important that this inappropriate conduct be evaluated by having both a mental and physical exam performed. The physical exam might uncover problems that are contributing to or causing the behavior, including the use of any medications. It is also essential that the issue be discussed with caregivers and that they be educated about what is appropriate and inappropriate. Social workers, physicians, nurses, and other healthcare professionals should be consulted on how best to deal with the situation.

CHAPTER 13

SENIOR SUBSTANCE ABUSE

"All diseases run into one, old age." —Ralph Waldo Emerson

---

ubstance abuse is defined as the use of chemical substances (alcohol or drugs, both legal and illegal) that lead to an increased risk of physical and mental problems and an inability to control the use of the substance.

Not generally known is the conclusion of the Centers for Disease Control's "Report on Binge Drinking" of January 2012: people sixty-five and older binge drink more often than any other age group. The National Institute on Alcohol Abuse and Alcoholism defines binge drinking "as a pattern of drinking that brings a person's blood alcohol concentration to 0.08 grams percent or above. This typically happens when men consume 5 or more drinks, and when women consume 4 or more drinks, in about 2 hours."

Another concerning statistic is this one from the Substance Abuse and Mental Health Services Administration: in 2008, the number of people fifty years and older who requested help for substance abuse was 231,200, up from 102,700 in 1992.

ALCOHOLISM

In the elderly population, alcoholism is becoming a significant and growing problem. It is misdiagnosed, under-treated or sometimes not even recognized. Only about one-third of primary care physicians routinely screen elderly patients for alcohol problems.

According to recent data, three million seniors have alcohol abuse disorders. In the United States, widowers over the age of seventy-five have the highest rate of alcoholism. Fewer women drink, but those who imbibe heavily have more severe consequences than men and are less likely to be diagnosed or receive treatment.

Lifestyle changes such as retirement, disability, death of a spouse, or a move from a much beloved home can cause grief and depression. In order to cope, some seniors self-medicate with drugs or alcohol. They often drink alone at home, successfully hiding their problem from friends and family. Alcohol is readily available and accessible for a senior. After all, with gray hair and a wrinkled face, what store clerk is going to ask for ID?

As we age, sensitivity to the effects of alcohol increases. The blood alcohol concentration is greater because of a decrease in total body water content. A dehydrated body loses its ability to adapt to the presence of alcohol. Women not only have lower total body water content than men of comparable weight but also have reduced stomach enzymes that help metabolize alcohol. A person can experience increasing difficulties as he or she ages even though drinking patterns remain unchanged from when he or she was younger. Add to this mix the more than 150 medications that interact negatively with alcohol and you have a potential health crisis in the making.

The effects of alcoholism are severe. High alcohol consumption impairs sleep patterns, interferes with required medications, and worsens medical conditions. It is a risk factor for several physical disorders, including stomach and liver problems, and contributes to depression, suicide, and brain dysfunction.

Alcoholic patients tend to have lower cancer survival rates. Certain cancers that already have an increasing age-related incidence (such as liver, colon, prostate, esophagus, and larynx cancer) are given a boost by alcoholism. Even women who are moderate drinkers experience an increase in breast cancer.

Older alcoholics are at risk for multiple falls, which can result in fractures, chronic subdural hematomas, debilitating injuries, and even death. Of course, taking a combination of medications and alcohol increases the likelihood of a fall.

The toxic effects of alcohol on the nervous system may cause brain damage with symptoms similar to Alzheimer's disease: short-term memory loss, confusion, diminished verbal fluency, and impaired problem solving skills. (See "Case Study" at the end of this chapter.)

DRUG ABUSE

According to testimony presented to Congress in 2012 by Dr. Nora Volkow of the National Institute on Drug Abuse, "Older Americans who currently make up only 13 percent of the population...receive approximately one-third of all medications prescribed in the Nation." She goes on to say that these prescribed drugs can negatively interact with over-the-counter medicines and dietary supplements, which seniors tend to consume in considerable quantities. The power of deceptive advertising! One of my clients bought, on average, four hundred dollars worth of vitamins every month. There was no convincing her that these vitamins were not effective and a waste of money.

In many situations, physicians prescribe drugs for a long period of time, which can lead to misuse or abuse (see the chapter on "Health Care Advocacy" regarding doctors' lack of attention to their elderly patients). The most commonly abused drugs are those prescribed for anxiety, sleep problems and pain management. The patient might not even realize that he or she is physically or emotionally dependent on a substance, or he or she may believe that addiction will not become an issue since the medication was prescribed. However, since older adults experience changes in metabolism and increased susceptibility to toxic effects, caretakers and health professionals need to be vigilant.

Many types of sleep aids can be extremely addicting and can lead to significant memory problems. In older people, these drugs may cause unusual or erratic behavior or lead to a persistent state of confusion.

Narcotics for pain management are called opioids and include Percocet, Vicodin, and Oxycontin. These drugs can successfully alleviate pain by disrupting the biological processes that lead to the feeling of pain. Even under strict medical supervision, the body can develop a tolerance for these types of drugs. When that occurs, more of the drug is required, leading to physical dependence and, invariably, to addiction at a mental and emotional level.

Benzodiazepines, which include Ativan, Valium, or Xanax, reduce activity in the brain so that the patient is less anxious, can sleep better, and is not as affected by distressing situations. When dosages are not properly managed, tolerance for the drug may develop and withdrawal symptoms could be experienced if the patient discontinues using the medication.

If your parent is living alone and is displaying signs of confusion or memory loss and taking several medications, it is critical that someone monitors the dosage and the use on a daily basis. In many cases, it is not only important to ensure that the proper amount of the drug is taken but also that it is taken at a certain time of day. Even if your parent is only using one or two medications, he or she may occasionally forget to take them on the prescribed basis. Pill dispensers can help with the prescription management process and are sold in drug stores or online. Some are available with an alarm system to alert the patient or caregiver that it is time to take the medication.

You can also hire someone to set up and dispense medications, thus ensuring that they are taken appropriately. Caregivers, social workers, or nurses can be employed to visit your parent on a regular basis and set up the medications that will be needed throughout the week. Check with your state's medical board or department of health to determine if a person needs special certification in order to actually give your parent his or her medication.

If you are concerned that your parent may be misusing drugs, look for the following symptoms:

- anxiety/agitation

- memory loss/confusion

- depression

- blood pressure changes

- pain in the upper abdomen

- fatigue/trouble sleeping

- appetite and weight loss

- weakness

- history of falling

As you can see, these symptoms mirror other health issues. Consult with your parent's physician to receive a correct diagnosis.

Once you suspect that your parent has an abuse problem, take action immediately by seeking the help of a social worker, doctor, or other healthcare professional. Many options can be pursued to assist the substance abuser and his or her family. These include individual, group, or family therapy; outpatient or inpatient rehab; family intervention; and participation in organizations such as Alcoholics Anonymous. Your local county social services, healthcare providers, and mental health facilities can offer referrals. For more information on alcohol and drug abuse, contact the following agencies:

- National Institute on Drug Abuse at
  www.drugabuse.gov or 301-443-1124

- Substance Abuse and Mental Health Services
  Administration at www.hhs.gov or 240-276-2000

Older adults may do better in substance abuse programs that are designed for people their age. For information on age-related programs pertaining to alcoholism, contact Seniors in Sobriety (SIS) at www.seniorsinsobriety.org.

Case Study: I witnessed the brain deterioration of a client due to alcoholism over several years. Initially, his driver's license was suspended for driving under the influence, but he continued to drive and was arrested again. He found himself spending a lot of money on an attorney to represent him in court to reduce his sentence. Of course, he thought nothing of showing up for his court dates with alcohol on his breath. After that, he got into a series of fights with the patrons of his local bar and was bounced permanently from the establishment. Subsequently, he proceeded to fall down a flight of stairs at a commuter train station and was arrested for intoxication. Following that incident, he set fire to his kitchen by turning on all the stove's burners and neglecting to remove a pan from one of those burners. His doctor warned him that his brain would turn into "mush" but, by then, he no longer had the mental capacity to take this warning seriously. He died at age seventy-seven but may have been able to live a longer, more rewarding life had it not been for his addiction.

CHAPTER 14
BE A LEGAL EAGLE

*"Do not regret growing older. It is a
privilege denied to many."* —Unknown

BEING PROACTIVE BEFORE
THE DEATH OF A PARENT

Adult children and their parents are notorious for skirting the issues relating to finances and dying. These subjects are often painful and embarrassing to discuss, and are often ignored.

For a parent, it is more likely a generational thing. The "older" generation does not feel that it's proper to burden their children with financial matters and with the legal ramifications of their inevitable demise. In other instances, some elderly people develop paranoia regarding money. They may take steps to ensure that their financial assets and distribution of those assets upon their death are kept secret. That is not to say that a parent should automatically share information with an adult child if that child's past behavior leads them to believe that their physical and financial health would be placed in jeopardy.

Adult children, especially those in a caretaking role, must be knowledgeable regarding their parent's bank and brokerage accounts, retirement benefits, and the existence of a will or trust. If the caretaker is not the executor of the estate, he or she needs to know whom to contact regarding health and financial decisions.

In some cases, an adult child is not made aware of his or her role as an executor until immediately before or after the death of a parent. Obviously, this puts that child at a disadvantage and leaves him or her little time to prepare for this important function.

Therefore, put aside your discomfort in talking about measures that have been taken in preparation for the distribution of your parent's estate. Explain that you want to ensure all of his or her wishes will be carried out and that it is of utmost importance to have these discussions before it's too late.

LOCATING IMPORTANT DOCUMENTS

If you are named as the executor of the estate, you should have a copy of the will or trust agreement and the name and contact information of the attorney who prepared it. You need to be proactive and find out the location of your parent's important documents, including:

- bank accounts

- brokerage, retirement, and pension accounts

- credit card accounts

- annuities

- property purchases, sales, and other transactions

- loans (those made to them or those they made to others)

- income tax returns

- deeds and titles to property (such as home and auto)

- property tax statements

- life and health insurance policies

- homeowners and automobile insurance policies

- birth certificate

- marriage certificate and/or divorce decree

- death certificate of spouse

- military service records

- funeral and burial arrangements

Talk with your parent about consolidating his or her financial accounts, which will prevent huge headaches for the executor of the estate. Many older people tend to open several checking or savings accounts. Sometimes this is at the suggestion of a bank employee who may be recommending it more for the bank's benefit than for the senior's. As is often the case, a senior might not trust having all his or her money in just one financial institution and believes it's better to "spread the wealth around." For assistance in consolidating brokerage, IRA, and other investment accounts, consult with an *independent* financial advisor.

Yes, it is a big job. That's why you need to get started now!

WILLS AND TRUSTS

(Laws governing wills and trusts may vary from state to state.)

Both wills and trusts are legal devices that can be used to provide for the distribution of an estate's assets. The decision about which device best suits an individual's circumstances should be made by conferring with an estate or an elder law attorney. The attorney's fees for setting up a will are usually less than for setting up a trust. There are online websites that offer "do-it-yourself" wills and trusts, but they do not provide legal advice, which could be critical to how the will or trust will hold up if challenged in court.

A *will* is a document that allows distribution of property to go to named beneficiaries and comes into play only after death. It is subject to probate, which means that the estate pays costs to the court to supervise the handling of the will, any beneficiary challenges, and creditor disputes. These costs are determined by the laws of the state in which the deceased resided and can be substantial. The terms of the will are entered into the public record at the time of death.

A *living trust* can be revocable, which means that changes can be made to it, or irrevocable, which means that changes cannot be made to it. The trust is used as a mechanism to manage property and assets before and after death, and it sets forth how those assets (and the income earned by the trust) are distributed upon death. Though a trust costs more to prepare, fund, and manage, there are no probate costs involved if all the grantor's assets are held by the trust.

A trust allows the grantor to manage the trust assets as long as he or she is willing and able to do so, and it makes provisions for a successor trustee to take over the asset management if the grantor relinquishes that duty. The trust is not subject to probate proceedings or to automatic court supervision. It does not automatically become a part of the public record.

Besides distribution of assets, another important component of a will or trust is the healthcare directive, also called a living will or healthcare power of attorney. This document advises the executor, doctor, or other medical service providers what actions should be taken regarding healthcare. It designates the type of treatment or non-treatment the patient wants in certain situations.

Over the years, much has been made of this topic in the media, and this is a good thing. Regardless of a person's age, debilitating illnesses or accidents can occur. It is important for all of us to let our family members know how we would like to be treated when we are unable to make healthcare decisions. In fact, even if a will or trust has not yet been completed, it is a very good idea to ensure that a healthcare directive has been issued. Contact your state's attorney general's office, a local hospital, or a physician for a form.

Dying without a will or trust is termed "dying intestate." If there is no will or trust, state law controls and distributes property to a spouse or closest heirs. The state can appoint anyone to be the administrator of the property, and the administrator may have to pay fees or post a bond at the expense of the estate before he or she can begin to distribute assets.

Now that you have had this brief tutorial on wills and trusts, you realize how critical it is to discuss the topic with your parent, especially if he or she has not yet made these legal preparations.

CHAPTER 15
CONSERVATORSHIPS

"Age is a question of mind over matter. If you don't mind, it doesn't matter." —Leroy "Satchel" Paige

---

WHY A CONSERVATORSHIP MAY BE NEEDED

(Laws governing conservatorships may vary from state to state.)

A conservatorship, or adult guardianship, is granted in cases where an incapacitated person can no longer make decisions regarding financial or healthcare issues. This incapacitation might be the result of dementia, a serious illness or injury, a coma, or the inability to manage financial assets due, for example, to an addiction. There are a number of people who can file for conservatorship, including the spouse or domestic partner, a relative, a state agency, other interested parties such as a friend, and even the proposed conservatee. For information on how to file for a conservatorship, call your local courthouse or seek the counsel of an attorney who specializes in this area of law. To find an attorney in your locality, contact your state's Bar Association or the National

Academy of Elder Law Attorneys at www.naela.org or call 703-942-5711.

After an application for conservatorship is filed, a judge hears evidence on the proposed conservatee's mental capacity. The court may also appoint an investigator to determine if there is a need for a conservator and, if so, to recommend a particular person to serve in that capacity. If family members, friends, or the proposed conservator objects to the conservatorship or to a choice of conservator, he or she must file papers with the court, advise all interested parties, and attend a legal hearing.

WHO CAN ACT AS A CONSERVATOR

Once the court determines that a conservator is needed, the court designates a person to act in that capacity. When the court appoints someone to take care of financial matters, that person is called a "conservator of the estate," while a person in charge of medical and personal decisions is called a "conservator of the person." The same person can be appointed to act in both capacities. These guardians are supervised and held accountable to the court.

The process of obtaining a conservatorship is lengthy. However, when a conservatorship is needed immediately, the court may appoint a temporary conservator. This person is responsible for the temporary care and protection of the conservatee's finances and property.

When choosing a conservator, most states give preference to the conservatee's spouse, domestic partner, adult children, adult siblings, or other blood relatives. It is unlikely that a non-relative would be appointed as conservator if there was a relative willing to serve. This is where family dynamics come in to play. If one relative is chosen by the court over another relative, be prepared for sparks to fly. Conservatorship proceedings can cause friction in family relationships and change family dynamics.

If a family member or friend is not available to serve as a conservator, an outside person who has expertise in the field of conservatorship, such as a public or private fiduciary, can be appointed (a fiduciary is a person who assumes responsibility for various positions of trust, such as managing and protecting money and property). Public fiduciaries, or public guardians, work in a government agency and are supported by taxpayer funding. Private fiduciaries charge hourly rates or a percentage of assets. Sometimes the court determines the fees on a case-by-case basis.

In situations where family dysfunction is an issue, you may want to consider a public or private fiduciary. Also, conservatorships can be time-consuming, often requiring court hearings, the continuing assistance of an attorney, and the tracking of detailed records and court documentation. A public or private fiduciary may be a good alternative to a family member or friend. The services of a private fiduciary can be costly, but if you or your parent has sufficient financial resources, using one may prevent a few Excedrin headaches.

The attorney handling the conservatorship or the court will be able to refer you to a fiduciary. In addition, you may contact your state's attorney general's office at www.naag.org, your local county social services, or search the Internet for professional fiduciary organizations in your area. The members of these organizations must meet certain educational requirements and standards.

As mentioned above, the conservator's role entails a lot of work as he or she must keep a variety of records and must file court papers on a regular basis. The conservator is subject to court supervision, which may require the conservator to receive permission from the court before making major decisions and to post a bond (a kind of insurance policy) that protects the conservatee's estate from mismanagement.

Conservators are generally reimbursed for expenses from the assets of the conservatee. Usually, compensation is only made to professional or public conservators, but a family member who has been appointed as conservator may also request compensation by applying to the court.

A conservator does not provide financial support for the conservatee. He or she only manages the conservatee's assets and makes decisions affecting the financial or personal well-being of the conservatee. A financial conservator is responsible for diligently ensuring that the conservatee is receiving all the benefits for which he or she may qualify, such as Social Security, medical insurance, retirement benefits, public assistance, and Veterans Administration benefits.

Once the court appoints a conservator, that person acts in this capacity until the court issues an order ending his or her responsibility. This usually happens when the conservatee dies, when the conservatee no longer needs this level of assistance, if the conservatee's assets have been depleted, or if the conservator resigns. In this last case, the court then appoints someone else to assume the conservator's duties.

CHAPTER 16

END OF LIFE—
HOSPICE CARE

*"You spend 90% of your adult life hoping
for a long rest and the last 10% trying
to convince the Lord that you're actually
not that tired." —Robert Brault*

TERMINAL ILLNESS AND
END-OF-LIFE ISSUES

One of the most difficult subjects (aside from financial and legal matters) for an adult child to discuss with their parent is that parent's end of life issues. We all want to believe that we will remain healthy and physically active until such time when we gently pass away in our sleep. Unfortunately, our life experiences and statistics do not support that hope.

Hospice is a program of care and support for people who are terminally ill. The program focuses on helping patients live comfortably by controlling pain and other symptoms, not on curing the illness. This care is administered by specially trained professionals and caregivers to ensure that the patient's physical, emotional, and spiritual needs are met.

Services may include not only physical care but also counseling, drugs, equipment, and supplies. Additionally, hospice programs provide continuing support for the family after a patient's death.

According to the National Hospice & Palliative Care Organization, an estimated 1.65 million patients received services from hospice in 2011. Approximately 45 percent of all deaths in the United States were under the care of a hospice program in that same year.

HOSPICE CARE

Not all hospice care is alike. To find the best service for your parent's needs, you should talk with your parent's doctor or other healthcare professionals, social workers, clergy, or friends who have received hospice care for a family member. The hospice care provider must be certified by Medicare in order for the patient to receive Medicare benefits for this service. For more information on finding a hospice program, you may contact:

- Hospice Foundation of America at 800-854-3402 or www.hospicefoundation.org

- National Hospice & Palliative Care Organization at 800-658-8898 or www.nhpco.org

- Hospice Association of America at 202-546-4759 or www.nahc.org/haa

- Medicare at www.medicare.gov or 800-633-4227

In order for your parent to receive hospice care, a coordinator from the hospice program will contact your parent's physician to ensure that hospice care is appropriate. Your parent's doctor and the hospice medical director will certify that your parent is terminally ill and has six months or less to live (this is a Medicare requirement). Hospice will assess your parent's needs, make recommendations on any special equipment that is required, and arrange to obtain the equipment. The hospice team will prepare an individualized care plan and will schedule regular visits.

Hospice care is usually provided in the patient's home. However, if the patient requires more care than can be provided in a home setting, some hospices have their own inpatient facilities. There are also nursing homes and hospitals with hospice care options. The hospice staff is on call for emergencies twenty-four hours a day, but the program *does not* include a nurse in the home twenty-four hours a day, seven days a week.

Initially, the patient may not require family members, friends, or paid caregivers to provide any assistance. However, as the patient's health deteriorates, it is recommended that someone be available to care for him or her on a continuous basis. Medicare does provide some home health care coverage but there are restrictions. Visit the website at www.medicare.gov and search under "home health care." If the patient does not qualify for Medicare's home health care services but has long-term care insurance, caregiving services will be paid by the insurance provider according to the plan's coverage.

Hospice neither hastens nor postpones dying but provides knowledgeable caregivers during the dying process. The hospice nurses and doctors are trained in the latest medications and devices for pain and symptom relief. It is their goal for the patient to be pain free and as alert as possible. If the patient's condition improves and it is determined that the disease is in remission, the patient can be discharged from hospice. Should the patient need to return to hospice care later on, Medicare and most private insurance will allow additional coverage for this purpose.

MEDICARE

All this care sounds wonderful but, of course, the cost can be extraordinary. And here we get to the crux of the matter. Hospice coverage is provided by Medicare nationwide (even if the patient is in a Medicare Advantage Plan or other Medicare health plan), by Medicaid in forty-seven states, and by most private insurance carriers. If the patient is covered under original Medicare, there is no cost to him or her. If the patient is not covered by Medicare or any other health insurance, some hospices will provide care by using funds raised from donations to foundations or memorial gifts. As Medicare and other insurance benefits can and do change, check with them before signing your parent up for a hospice care program.

Medicare hospice benefits are received when the patient meets the following conditions:

- He or she is eligible for Medicare Part A (see chapter titled "Medicare & More").

- A doctor and the hospice medical director have certified that he or she is terminally ill and has six months or less to live.

- The care received is from a Medicare approved hospice program.

- The patient signs a statement choosing hospice care instead of other Medicare-covered benefits to treat his or her terminal illness (Medicare will continue to pay for any covered health problems that are not related to the terminal disease).

Medicare covers the following services and needs:

- a one-time only hospice consultation with a hospice medical director or hospice doctor to discuss care options and pain and symptom management

- nursing care, physician and social worker services

- medical equipment and supplies

- drugs (a small co-payment may be required)

- hospice aide and homemaker services

- physical and occupational therapy, dietary counseling, grief counseling

- respite care in a Medicare approved facility if the patient's primary caregiver needs a rest (it can be provided more than once but only on an occasional basis with a stay of up to five days each time; a small co-pay may be required)

Once hospice care is chosen, Medicare will not cover any treatment or drugs intended to cure the terminal illness, room and board in a nursing home or hospice facility, emergency room service, or ambulance transportation *unless* it is arranged by the hospice team or is unrelated to the terminal illness. Before your parent receives any of these services, the hospice team should be consulted. Otherwise, your parent might have to pay the entire cost.

As hospice care is intended for people with six months or less to live, the hospice medical director or hospice doctor will be required to recertify that the patient is terminally ill if he or she lives longer than six months. Hospice care is given in benefit periods. A patient can receive hospice care for two ninety-day periods followed by an unlimited number of sixty-day periods. At the beginning of each period, the hospice medical director or hospice doctor must recertify that the patient is terminally ill.

If a patient's health improves or the illness goes into remission, hospice care can be discontinued. Also, the patient has the right to withdraw from hospice at any time for any reason. Once the patient stops hospice care, his or her coverage will revert back to his or her original Medicare plan. The patient can go back to hospice care if he or she is deemed eligible.

For more information on hospice Medicare coverage, visit www.medicare.gov or call 800-633-4227.

CHAPTER 17
HEALTH CARE ADVOCACY

*"You know you're getting old when
all the names in your black book have
M.D. after them." —Arnold Palmer*

ENSURING APPROPRIATE AND EXPERT MEDICAL ATTENTION

After all the trips that your parent made with you to the doctor for vaccinations and various childhood illnesses, holding your hand and trying to soothe you when that big needle came your way, it is now payback time. Since your parent's physical and mental well-being is crucial to living an independent lifestyle, you will have to be vigilant to ensure that the medical professionals are paying close attention.

Many elderly patients only hear what they want to hear from the doctor, conveniently "forgetting" any advice or diagnosis that does not fit in with their reality. They also may not recall some or all of the doctor's instructions due to either denial or memory loss. They may have no idea what was discussed because of hearing problems—but they won't admit it.

Frankly, most doctors and hospital facilities are intimidating. Once a person starts losing his or her eyesight, hearing, and mental alertness, the healthcare professionals and medical jargon become even more daunting.

Unfortunately, doctors may be just as much at fault. From my experience, I discovered that many doctors who treat elderly patients brush off symptoms and ailments by attributing them to "old age." Some doctors spend little time with the patient, thereby not noticing symptoms that should be addressed. It is amazing how the doctor's approach and demeanor changes if another person accompanies the patient into the exam room and starts jotting down notes.

When you become aware of a decline in your parent's memory, hearing, or eyesight, and when he or she gives vague answers about what transpired during a visit to the doctor, it is time for you or another responsible adult to accompany your parent to all medical appointments. Come prepared with questions, notepaper, and pen. This makes it clear to the medical provider that you are serious about keeping abreast of your parent's heath conditions.

Mom or Dad probably will not appreciate your interference with the doctor/patient relationship. Calmly explain that his or her health could be at risk and you want to ensure the best medical attention is being provided. If your parent balks at your "meddling," write a letter to the doctor addressing the health matters that are causing your concern. Due to privacy regulations, the doctor may not be willing to discuss these matters with you, but at least he or she will be aware of problems that are not being communicated by your parent.

To circumvent these privacy laws, the healthcare provider or medical facility can give your parent a consent form that allows you or another responsible party to consult with them about your parent's medical issues. The only catch: your parent has to sign it.

GERIATRIC SPECIALISTS

If you want to make your life less stressful, consider the options of geriatric healthcare providers and geriatric social workers. These are professionals who have had special training in dealing with the elderly population (the definition of geriatric is "of, or relating to, the aged or the aging process").

The main goal of geriatric medicine is to promote the well-being of the aging patient. This sector of the population tends to have unique health problems, with multiple health issues often occurring at the same time.

In the United States, a doctor must be board certified in either internal medicine or family practice in order to specialize in geriatrics. Additionally, the doctor undergoes advanced training in order to receive certification in the field. Besides geriatric physicians, there are nurses, physical therapists, social workers, psychiatrists, and nutritionists who are certified in geriatrics and who can also assist in supporting the patient's health.

To find a geriatric doctor or other healthcare specialist in your area, contact your state's medical board, local hospitals, county social service agencies, or other physicians. Also, you may go online and search "geriatric doctors/physicians" or visit the website of the Federation of State Medical Boards at www.fsmb.org.

For families who find themselves in a caregiving situation, the geriatric social worker could become your new best friend. These social workers are an invaluable resource.

They know what agencies to contact regarding any number of senior issues and how to navigate through these agencies to attain the best result for their client. Some geriatric social workers are nurses or other medical professionals who have sophisticated medical knowledge.

The social worker is your liaison between healthcare staff, social services, and government agencies. He or she can also communicate on your behalf with out-of-the-loop siblings and other relatives. The social worker often acts as a buffer between family members. For example, those siblings who like to push each other's "emotional buttons" will often discover their manipulative technique is ineffective with a social worker.

Some of the areas in which the geriatric social worker can assist include:

- advocating for the patient—from doctors to caregivers, a geriatric social worker can ensure that the best possible help is being provided and will report any suspected elder abuse to adult protective services

- providing a plan of care with specific recommendations after assessing the senior's needs and his/her ability to function

- finding solutions that enhance the quality of life of the client, such as arranging activities and group outings

- delivering public or private services that are available for the client and the family

- coordinating the discharge of the client from hospital to home and ensuring that the client has all necessary medical and caregiving assistance that is required

Yes, the fees a private social worker charges can be expensive. However, if you consider the time it would take for you to do all the legwork and research, and also the resulting frustration, hiring a social worker will often prove to be a very worthwhile investment.

When seeking the services of a geriatric social worker, ask for license information, experience, training, and references. Discuss the social worker's care philosophy. For instance, what are his or her feelings about home care versus assisted living? Under what circumstances would he or she resign from the case? The social worker should provide you with a written contract that details the charges for each of the different services he or she will provide.

To find a geriatric social worker and get more information on standards that have been set for this field, you may contact the chapter of the National Association of Social Workers (NASW) in your state or visit www.socialworkers.org. You may also contact the National Association of Professional Geriatric Care Managers at www.caremanager.org or county social services, doctors, and hospitals.

CHAPTER 18
ACTIVE SENIOR OPTIONS

"To keep the heart unwrinkled, to be hopeful,
kindly, cheerful, reverent—that is to triumph
over old age." —Thomas Bailey Aldrich

A s some people age, they may be more inclined to stay within the confines of their home because they fear that their physical or mental limitations prevent them from associating with other people. You may have a parent who has never been a social butterfly or you may have one who managed to be the president of every club to which he or she belonged. For both the parent who has become a recluse due to infirmities and for the parent who still wants to maintain an active social life, adult day care centers or senior centers may provide a good outlet.

ADULT DAY CARE CENTERS

Adult day care centers are for those seniors who cannot manage independently or who are isolated and lonely. These centers enable seniors to socialize while still receiving needed care services and also offer main caregivers a respite from caregiving responsibilities. Adult day care centers provide programs that are designed to generate well-being in the senior through social and health-related services. Along with special activity programs, many offer nutritious meals and may be able to accommodate special diets. Typically, they operate during daytime hours, Monday through Friday.

Most adult day care centers function with a staff that includes an activity director and assistants, a social worker, a registered nurse or licensed practical nurse, and a center director. Those that serve a large number of participants may also employ a driver to transport participants to and from the center.

Each state has different regulations for the operation of adult day care centers, although the National Adult Day Services Association (NADSA) offers some overall guidelines. The NADSA recommends a minimum staff-to-participant ratio of one staff member to every six seniors. If the center deals with a significant number of seniors who have high levels of physical or mental impairment, this ratio may be even lower.

Some activities that are provided by adult day care services include arts and crafts, musical programs, mental stimulation, exercise programs, discussion groups, local outings, and holiday and birthday celebrations. In addition, some centers offer transportation to and from the center, have counseling and support groups for caregivers, and provide health services such as blood pressure monitoring and vision screening.

An adult day care center may be a good choice for your parent if your parent is isolated but desires companionship, can no longer structure his or her own daily activities, or cannot be safely left alone at home. Appropriate candidates for adult day care centers are seniors who are mobile (but may use a cane, walker, or wheelchair), are in the early stages of dementia, will derive benefit from social contact, may have physical or cognitive issues but do not require twenty-four-hour supervision, and are continent (in most cases).

Participation in an adult day care center does require a fee. These centers need funding to provide meals, activities, transportation, and healthcare supervision. The average cost is about sixty-four dollars per day, according to www. helpguide.org.

The actual cost will depend upon the location of the center and the services it offers. Medicare does not pay for adult day care centers, although Medicaid will pay most or all of the costs of licensed adult day *healthcare* centers for participants with very low incomes and few assets. An adult day *healthcare* center provides physical, occupational, and speech therapy and usually requires a medical assessment by a doctor before someone is admitted into the program.

For help in paying for the cost of participation in an adult day care center, contact your parent's private medical insurance and long-term care insurance carriers. Also, be sure to inquire about financial assistance when talking with center personnel.

To find a center in your area, check with your local social services or health department, mental health centers, local senior center, or family physician. You can also contact the Administration for Community Living at www.acl.gov or call 202-619-0724.

Once you have found a center, try to spend a few hours there so that you can get an idea of how the center is operated. There are a number of things you should look for while visiting the center, both generally and specifically as it relates to your parent.

Is the center clean? Does it have wheelchair accessibility? Do the staff members have good attitudes? What activities are offered? Is transportation provided? What are the credentials of the staff members? What is the ratio of staff members to participants? Are meals included? What kind of physical or mental impairments are not accepted?

Ask for references and talk to others who have used the center. Find out who owns or sponsors the center, if it is licensed or certified, and how long it has been operating.

SENIOR CENTERS

Senior centers offer active seniors a place in their community where they can socialize and participate in a variety of activities. These can include bus trips to events and places of interest, classes, and exercise programs. Centers may hold special luncheons where they invite speakers to address problems encountered by the aging community. In addition, senior centers may provide assistance with government programs such as Medicare, veteran's benefits, and income tax return preparation.

Most centers are run by local governments but cooperate with other agencies in the area. They rely heavily on donations and on volunteers who assist the paid staff with programs and services.

The age requirement for a senior to qualify for admission varies by location, but, in general, the average age is between fifty-five and sixty. Usually, a small fee is required for membership, plus extra charges for special activities. Those seniors on a limited income may be able to receive a reduction in fees.

Not all senior centers are alike, and large cities may have more than one. If you have the time, it would be a good idea for you and your parent to visit the senior center in order to determine if the environment and staff are a good fit.

Do not confuse senior centers with senior or retirement communities. Those communities provide housing for seniors and, although they may provide activities for their residents, they are not senior centers.

To find a senior center nearest your parent's home, check with the city hall, the county's social services, the phone directory, or online.

CHAPTER 19

ORGANIZATION—THE KEY TO SUCCESS

"Middle age is when you have a choice of two temptations and choose the one that will get you home earlier." —Unknown

---

D ealing with your personal and work-related concerns, as well as those issues generated by your parent, is no small feat. In fact, it can be downright overwhelming and stressful. If you are not an organized individual in the first place, taking on another person's paperwork can be disastrous. Because your parent's financial and physical health is at stake, this is no time to "wing it."

There are professionals who have expertise in paying bills, reconciling medical expenses with insurance payments, preparing taxes, investigating financial fraud, and organizing documentation. If you or your parent can afford it, I strongly suggest that you seek the help of these professionals. You can get referrals through your local county social services, senior centers, social workers, hospital social services, and your parent's accountant.

ORGANIZING DOCUMENTS AND RECORDS

If you do elect to take on the job, here are some tried (by me) and true helpful hints:

- Create a filing system for your parent's paperwork but *do not* comingle his or her paperwork with yours. See "Guidelines to Setting up a Filing System" in the Appendix.

- Retain only those records that are absolutely necessary. See "Recommended Records Retention Guidelines" in the Appendix. When discarding documents, ensure that those which include sensitive personal information (such as bank, credit card and brokerage account numbers, Social Security number, etc.,) are shredded. If there is a large amount of paperwork that requires shredding, take it to a self-serve shredding station or call a shredding service to come to the home. These services will shred on-site or will take the paperwork to an off-site location. Before employing a shredding service, ask for certification as to the legitimacy of the company.

- Keep the current year's paperwork in a file box or cabinet that is easily accessible.

- Documentation that needs to be retained but is over a year old should be stored in boxes that are labeled with dates and content information, and placed in a dry location—not out in the tool shed.

PAYING BILLS

- Your parent or the caregiver should place all incoming mail in a container (shoebox, tray, etc.,) for you to review on a weekly basis; you might also need to conduct a periodic search of your parent's home to ensure that mail has not been mislaid.

- Keep a list of those bills that are paid on a regular/ monthly basis and use that list to ensure that you are receiving them in a timely manner.

- To reduce bill-paying time and guarantee that critical bills are being paid, set up automatic payments with the water, power, phone, garbage, and credit card companies. To set up these automatic payments, contact the companies to request an authorization form (some companies will set up automatic payments over the phone). These payments can be made by using a bank account or credit card. Your parent will continue to receive statements from the companies, but these statements will note that payment is being made automatically.

- Pay bills as they come in so you will not forget to do so. If some bills cannot be paid immediately because of lack of funds in the checking account, set up a reminder file by month and date due, and insert the bill in the appropriate month's section.

- After the bill has been paid, note the date paid, amount paid, and check number on the statement or invoice, and file it. See "Guidelines to Setting Up a Filing System" in the Appendix.

- Keep the checkbook register updated with
  the check number, date issued, to whom
  it was issued, and the amount.

- Reconcile the checkbook register with the
  checking account statement once a month.

MEDICAL BILLING RECONCILIATION

- Create a manual or computer spreadsheet to
  track medical bills and insurance payments.
  See the sample form "Medical Billing
  Reconciliation" in the Appendix.

- A spreadsheet should be created for each medical
  provider and for each patient (if you are tracking
  medical bills for both parents, each parent should have
  his or her own spreadsheet for each medical provider).

- When a medical invoice is received, note the date
  of service and the amount billed on the spreadsheet.
  The invoice may include the amount written
  off or paid by Medicare and any supplemental
  insurance payment that has been made. The medical
  provider usually only sends the patient a bill
  after all insurances have paid. To ensure that the
  medical provider has applied the correct insurance
  payment amounts, reconcile these amounts with the
  Medicare and supplemental insurance statements.

- As soon as you receive notice that all insurances
  have paid for the service, enter the amounts paid
  and the dates paid on the spreadsheet. Medicare will
  only send benefit statements every three months

unless the patient is being directly reimbursed for a service by Medicare. This will happen when a medical provider does not accept assignment from Medicare. The supplemental insurance statement will also note the amount Medicare has paid. If a patient is on Medicaid and uses a medical service provider who accepts Medicaid, there is no billing involved between the healthcare provider and the patient.

- Once all insurance payments have been made (usually directly to the medical service provider), you can then pay any remaining balance. On the spreadsheet, input the amount of the balance paid under "patient payment" and the date paid.

- Some medical providers may send several bills for the same service date until all payments by the insurance companies have been made (or not made, if the service was not covered). Do not be intimidated by the continuing receipt of bills. You should not pay a medical bill until both Medicare and the supplemental insurance company have made payment or issued a reason as to why they did not. If you have questions about a bill or about insurance payments, do not hesitate to call the medical provider's billing department, Medicare, or the supplemental insurance company.

CREDIT PROTECTION

- One free credit report per year can be requested from each of the reporting agencies: Equifax, Experian,

and TransUnion. To receive the reports, visit www.
annualcreditreport.com or call the reporting agencies:
  Equifax: 800-685-1111
  Experian: 888-397-3742
  TransUnion: 800-916-8800

- On at least a yearly basis, request credit reports
  for your parent and review carefully for fraudulent
  activity. If a credit problem exists due to some form
  of identity theft, you will need to request reports on
  a continuing basis until the problem is resolved.

- Enroll your parent in a credit protection program.
  Choose one that not only monitors credit activity
  but also *prevents* a criminal from opening an
  account using your parent's private information.

- Scrutinize in detail all credit card, bank, and
  investment statements for unusual activity.
  Report this activity by phone immediately to the
  financial institution and follow up your verbal
  communication with written correspondence. This
  creates a paper trail in the event the problem is not
  addressed properly by the financial institution.

- If you do not receive a response, or the problem
  is not resolved to your satisfaction, contact
  your state's attorney general's office or your
  local district attorney's office. Or, call the
  Consumer Finance Protection Bureau at 855-
  411-2372 or visit www.consumerfinance.com.

- One agency that helps to resolve disputes with banks
  and/or credit card companies is the Office of the

Comptroller of the Currency. This agency's primary mission is to charter, regulate, and supervise all national banks and federal savings associations. It oversees these financial institutions to ensure fair treatment of their customers and fair access to credit and financial products. You may call the Office of the Comptroller of the Currency at 800-613-6743 or visit the website at www.occ.treas.gov. Having dealt with this agency in a credit card fraud case, I can attest to its efficiency and effectiveness.

● If your parent is the victim of identity theft, the Federal Trade Commission (FTC) suggests immediately taking the following steps:

1. Place a fraud alert with *one* of the credit reporting companies.
2. Consider requesting a credit freeze with *each* credit-reporting company. This will prevent potential creditors from accessing credit reports. Before doing this, you should contact your state attorney general's office to determine if there is a fee for freezing the credit file and how long the freeze can stay in effect. Visit the website of the National Association of Attorneys General at www.naag.org to find the office contact information for your state.
3. Order a credit report from *each* credit-reporting company.
4. Create an identity theft report by submitting a complaint to the FTC and filing a police report. For more information, contact the FTC at www.ftc.gov/idtheft or call 877-438-4338.

They have published a very comprehensive guide, "Taking Charge—What To Do If Your Identity is Stolen." Even if identity theft is not yet a problem, this is a good booklet to keep on hand. You may find this guide at your local library or you can contact the FTC at the above website or phone number.

CHAPTER 20
LETTING YOUR PARENT GROW OLD

"Wrinkled was not one of the things I wanted
to be when I grew up." —Unknown

ADULT CHILDREN'S REACTIONS TO THE AGING OF PARENTS

Most adult children carry an unchanging picture in their minds of their parents shepherding them from school to after-school activities, holding their head over the toilet bowl during flu season and nagging them to complete their homework. When graying hair, deep wrinkles, and infirmities begin to make their appearance, children many times cannot accept the fact that their parent is aging. It is difficult to acknowledge their parent's mortality and even more difficult to face their own. (The family members of one of my clients were aghast when she stopped dying her hair and "went gray" at age ninety-five. She wasn't old enough to have gray hair!)

We want to believe that our parent is still active and vibrant. We may drag Mom or Dad to social activities in which he or she does not want to participate or is not equipped to handle. Even if we don't accuse our parent outright of malingering, we might suggest it in our attitude and actions. (Does this sound familiar? You are probably remembering how your parent treated you as a teenager!) We may laugh at or dismiss our parent's complaints and requests for assistance, such as when he or she requests the use of a walker or wheelchair.

Here's a newsflash: the body starts the aging process while still in the womb. Since heredity plays an important part, not everyone will age at the same rate but no one will be able to escape getting old. No matter how many Botox injections or facelifts are performed, by the time the body hits fifty years old, physiological changes have already taken place, even though they may not initially be that noticeable.

DISEASES AND IMPAIRMENTS OF THE AGING POPULATION

As someone ages, there are a number of changes that affect various bodily functions:

- Cardiovascular system—The heart rate becomes slightly slower and the heart might become larger; blood vessels and arteries become less flexible, causing the heart to work harder to pump blood through them. This can lead to high blood pressure and other related problems. *Atherosclerosis* (the buildup of fatty deposits in blood vessels) can lead to a heart attack. *Arteriosclerosis* (a hardening of the arteries caused by fatty accumulations in the blood vessels) may cause strokes.

- Bones and joints—*Osteoporosis:* a bone disease that is most common in women, caused by changes in calcification of bones. It can cause upper and

lower back pain, impaired mobility, an elevated risk
of fracture, poor posture, and muscle weakness.
Osteoarthritis: a joint disease that involves
degeneration of cartilage and the growth of bony
lumps on fingers and knuckle joints. *Rheumatoid
arthritis:* an autoimmune disease that causes
chronic inflammation of the joints and may also
cause inflammation and injury in other organs.

- Muscles—There is a loss of strength and flexibility
  that may create balance and coordination problems.

- Digestive system—Constipation is more common
  in elderly adults due to a low-fiber diet, not drinking
  enough liquids, lack of exercise, and as a side effect of
  medications or medical conditions such as diabetes.

- Skin—Due to a decrease in the production of natural
  oils, the skin can become drier, thinner, and less
  elastic; bruising may become more prevalent.

- Respiratory system—Loss of muscle cells due
  to aging decreases the strength of the muscles
  associated with breathing; cartilage that connects
  the ribs to the sternum may become hardened or
  calcified making it more difficult for the rib cage to
  contract and expand normally. Inability to breathe
  properly may lead to low oxygenation of the blood.

- Teeth—Gums may recede from the teeth and certain
  medications can cause dry mouth, making the teeth
  and gums more susceptible to decay and infection.

- Eyesight—The lens of the eye hardens. This may result
  in a person's reduced ability to focus on close objects.

An older person's eyes may become more sensitive to light. *Cataracts* may affect the eye's lens and cause clouded vision. Age-related *macular degeneration* is the leading cause of severe vision loss in people over sixty. There are two types: dry and wet. Both are caused by the degeneration of the retina. Dry macular degeneration causes vision loss in the center of the field of vision. It generally progresses more slowly than the wet version. Wet macular degeneration, caused by blood vessels growing under the retina in the back of the eye that leak blood and fluid, is the more severe form of the disease. *Glaucoma* is a disease that causes an increase of pressure inside the eyeball, resulting in a progressive loss of peripheral vision.

- Hearing—Age may cause a decline in a person's ability to hear certain frequencies; higher frequencies may be more affected than mid or lower frequencies.

- Bladder and urinary tract—Loss of bladder control or incontinence can be attributed to medical conditions such as diabetes, enlarged prostate, or menopause; less blood flowing through the kidneys can create a reduction in kidney function and the resulting inability to produce urine; diminished muscle tone in the bladder can result in an inability to empty the bladder completely.

- Weight—Muscle mass decreases and body fat starts to take its place; fat tissue burns fewer calories than muscle, so caloric intake must decrease in order to maintain a healthy weight.

- Memory—It may take longer to learn new things or remember familiar names or words. (See the chapter titled "Is It Dementia or Is It Alzheimer's?")

By not taking your parent's physical or mental health conditions seriously, you will increase his or her anxiety and potentially make the situation worse. Acknowledge your parent's limitations but also provide him or her with support. Encourage your parent to pursue avenues that will let them take advantage of the things that he or she *can* do.

If your parent has a need for assistance to regain muscle tone and fitness, talk to the family physician about occupational and/or physical therapy, or ask for a referral to a personal trainer who has experience working with the geriatric set. Occupational therapists can assist seniors with everyday activities. They can be especially helpful in supporting older adults who have experienced physical or cognitive changes. For those who have had injuries or illnesses, physical therapists can help improve their movement and help manage their pain. A personal trainer can provide the senior with age-appropriate exercises and can monitor an exercise program for the older adult. Some therapists and trainers make house calls, which is convenient for those seniors who have trouble arranging for transportation.

The aging process cannot be stopped; however, its impact may be minimized. You should ensure that your parent makes healthy choices, takes advantage of programs that promote exercise and good nutrition, and seeks the care of health professionals who cater to the older population.

No matter how much family or religious support a senior receives, the process of aging is painful both physically and emotionally. If you ignore or dismiss the effects of your parent's aging process, your denial will negatively impact everyone. As a client once told me, "You get old by yourself. Getting old is lonely."

CHAPTER 21

A PENNY SAVED IS A PENNY EARNED

"Growing old is no more than a bad habit which a busy man has no time to form." — Andri Maurois

———————

I have worked with clients who are wealthy but think they have no money. I have worked with clients who live from one Social Security check to another, but, as long as they have enough credit cards with sky-high limits, do not have a care in the world. Regardless of whether your parent falls into one of these categories or is somewhere in the middle, it is always a worthwhile endeavor to find ways to save a few dollars whenever and wherever possible.

TIPS ON SAVING MONEY

Listed below are some different avenues to pursue in order for your parent to put more cash in his or her wallet.

Be aware that places offering senior discounts differ in determining what age constitutes a senior. Discounts may be applicable to those who are as young as fifty, but most are for those sixty or older. Offering proof of age, such as a driver's license or state identification card, will usually be required.

Unclaimed Property

Your parent may have assets that are being held by the state. These could include income tax refunds, a "forgotten" bank account, and payments from entities (in the form of checks) that were never cashed. Over the years, I have been able to assist clients in reclaiming property totaling more than eight thousand dollars. Visit the website of your state's controller or treasury office, or call them for instructions and the forms necessary to request unclaimed property. If your parent's spouse is deceased, check for unclaimed property under the deceased's name. Also, check for unclaimed property in all states in which your parent has resided.

Medical Expenses

As previously mentioned, it is critical that medical bills are reconciled with medical insurance payments (see "Medical Billing Reconciliation Form" in the Appendix). This will prevent your parent from paying more than he or she should for healthcare services. If you have questions about a medical provider's invoice, or if you receive a denial by an insurance company for payment of services, do not hesitate to contact them to resolve the matter. In many cases, this will result in substantial savings.

Many people do not have insurance coverage for dental services since dental insurance premiums, along with co-pays and limits on the amount of coverage, rarely make carrying this type of insurance worthwhile. However, many dentists offer a discount to their senior patients so be sure to ask your parent's dentist about his/her discount policy.

Taxes

Contact your parent's county tax collector to determine eligibility for an exemption or reduction in certain parcel taxes that may be available to homeowners who are 65 or older.

Utility Services

Most utility companies have reduced rates for seniors or for those seniors with low incomes. These services include electric/gas, water, garbage and telephone. Usually, an application will need to be completed. When applying for low-income rates, proof of eligibility may be required, such as a copy of a tax return.

Note: Check with the gas/electric company about "time-of-use" service or usage during "on peak" and "off peak" hours. The company may offer reduced rates during "off peak hours," (i.e. after 7 p.m. during the week or all hours on weekends). In other words, if your parent does large loads of laundry during "off peak" instead of "on peak" hours, he or she can save a significant amount of money.

Financial Services

Be diligent about reviewing credit card, bank, and other financial statements. If you suspect fraud, report it immediately to the financial institution and ensure that you follow up your verbal report with written correspondence. Contacting law enforcement and other agencies may be required (see the chapter titled "Organization—The Key to Success").

If a credit card company charges a yearly service fee, call them and request that the fee be removed. If they deny the request, consider applying for a new card with no annual fee and closing the other account. *Important*: Before closing a credit card account, ensure that any automatic charges are transferred to the new card.

Contact your parent's bank regarding accounts that offer free services or low fees for seniors. If a bank is charging a "minimum balance" fee for an account, consider closing that account and moving the money to another bank that does not charge such a fee. *Important*: Do not close the old account until all automatic deposits and debits have been moved to the new one.

If your parent's portfolio of investments is not currently being managed by an *independent* financial advisor, contact one and have them review the portfolio. Many will offer this service free of charge. It is often possible to receive a better return on investment while paying lower management fees.

Senior Memberships

There are several organizations that offer memberships (for a fee) to seniors and provide discounts for travel, shopping, dining, cell phones, and so forth. Two of the most nationally recognized are the American Association of Retired Persons

(AARP) at www.aarp.org or 888-687-2277 and the American Seniors Association (ASA) at www.americanseniors.org or 800-951-0017. The ASA touts itself as a more "conservative answer to AARP." Other organizations can be found on the Internet.

Subscriptions

If your parent is currently receiving magazine or news-paper subscriptions, be sure to ask about senior discounts. Track the number of subscriptions your parent is receiving to ensure they are really of interest to your parent and are not duplicated. Magazines and newspapers target seniors over the phone and by mail, realizing that seniors often have a difficult time saying "no."

Insurance

Take the time to review homeowner, earthquake, automobile, medical, and umbrella* insurance policies to determine if your parent has adequate insurance coverage at an affordable rate. Or, contact an insurance broker (check the Internet, phone book, or ask a friend for a reference). A broker is an independent agent who represents the buyer rather than an insurance company and tries to find the buyer the best policy at the best price.

---

*   *Umbrella insurance is designed to give added liability protection above and beyond the limits on homeowner, auto, and watercraft personal insurance policies. With an umbrella policy, depending on the insurance company, an additional one to five million dollars in liability protection can be added. This protection is designed to kick in when the liability on other current policies has been exhausted.*

If your parent is driving very little, or not at all, or should not be driving due to health conditions, selling the car creates big savings on gas, insurance, and maintenance costs. Plus, you will be able to sleep at night!

Charitable Giving

Your parent is constantly bombarded with phone calls and junk mail asking for donations. Aren't we all? As people age, they have a tendency to say "yes" to every caller, whipping out their credit card and providing the credit card number to the stranger on the other end of the line. Or, they will studiously go through all the donation requests that come through the mail and, without hesitation, write a check to each one. I have worked with several seniors and their families to assist in tracking the seniors' expenses. Their children have often been amazed by the amount of money going to charities—some of which may be less legitimate than others.

If your parent is still cognizant of financial matters, sit down with them for a chat about the amount of money that he or she can afford to donate and the types of charities in which he or she is most interested (for free evaluations and ratings of charities, visit the Charity Navigator website at www.charitynavigator.org). Then, draw up a list of charities, along with the amount your parent has agreed will be donated *annually* to each one. Make the contributions just *once* a year in December—no matter how many phone calls or mailings requesting donations are received in the interim.

Advise your parent not to give out a credit card number over the phone to solicitors (this is easier said than done). Emphasize that a phone caller may be a scammer and the credit card number could be used to purchase a trip to Italy for a total stranger instead of making a donation to a worthwhile cause.

If your parent is suffering from forgetfulness or the onset of dementia, it is a good idea to put the checkbook and credit cards in a place that is not easily accessible to him or her, or (better yet) to remove them from the home entirely. Of course, this may not go over well with your parent. He or she will probably interpret this action as one more instance of losing financial independence, or as a move to take financial control. To allay these fears, have discussions with your parent about identity theft and how his or her financial health could be placed in jeopardy. Also, let your parent know that he or she can use the checkbook and credit cards for shopping or other outings; then ensure you provide your parent with a trustworthy "companion" to assist him or her during these excursions.

Travel/Dining/Shopping

Many websites provide listings of companies that offer senior discounts; however, in most cases, they require a membership fee. Since this chapter is about how to save money, and since companies are always changing their discount policies, I would suggest that you create your own list of companies, stores, and so forth that your parent frequently patronizes. The following types of companies might be included in that listing:

- airlines

- rental car companies

- hotels

- restaurants

- grocery outlets

- retail stores

Phone the establishments or review their websites to determine the current discount percentage, the age minimum, the days and hours of the week the discount is available, and what restrictions apply. Also, make a note of the type of identification the senior must provide to receive the discount. Review this listing at least every six months to ensure its accuracy.

Other

Your local county social services, senior centers, and social workers can provide referrals to other miscellaneous services that offer discounts to seniors or to low-income seniors.

CHAPTER 22

MEDICAL EQUIPMENT AND DEVICES FOR SENIOR SAFETY

"The elderly don't drive that badly;
they're just the only ones with time to
do the speed limit." —Jason Love

"That [senior citizen] driver has nowhere to go
and all day to get there!" —Bruce Harrison

In order to keep your senior as active as possible while still keeping her or him safe and secure, there are several available devices and types of equipment that can assist in this regard. Some of these items, considered "durable medical equipment," are covered by Medicare and supplemental insurance if they are deemed medically necessary. A doctor's written prescription is required. To determine what items are covered, review the Medicare handbook, "Medicare & You," or Medicare's website at www.medicare.gov.

Medicare pays for different kinds of durable medical equipment in different ways: some equipment may be rented while other equipment may have to be purchased. Medicare will only cover equipment from a Medicare-approved supplier. If the supplier does not accept assignment from Medicare, it is not bound by Medicare cost limitations.

Currently, the patient pays 20 percent of the amount approved by Medicare. Usually, the supplemental insurance provider will reimburse the patient that 20 percent. If Medicare doesn't cover the equipment, the patient may choose to rent or buy the equipment and pay for it out of pocket. Your parent may be able to deduct these out of pocket expenses on his or her income tax return. Medical equipment, such as wheelchairs or walkers, is often donated to hospitals and thrift stores and can be purchased at substantial savings.

The IRS requires that deductible medical expenses are incurred "primarily to alleviate or prevent a physical or mental defect or illness." This means that equipment used to benefit general health is not deductible. Durable medical equipment must meet IRS requirements in order to be deductible. Walkers, crutches, hearing aids, wheelchairs, and hospital beds are examples of durable medical equipment. To ascertain deductibility, check with your parent's CPA or visit the Internal Revenue Service website at www.irs.gov to review Publications 502 ("Medical and Dental Expenses") and 554 ("Tax Guide for Seniors").

AVAILABLE PRODUCTS TO ASSIST WITH VISION, HEARING, AND MOBILITY LOSSES

Listed below by category (vision, hearing, physical mobility, and monitoring) are some examples of medical equipment and devices that may enhance your parent's lifestyle. For other suggestions, and for help in deciding which item is best for your senior's needs, discuss your senior's situation with healthcare professionals such as physical and occupational therapists, doctors, and social workers. These same professionals should be able to refer you to local suppliers, or you can search the Internet or the phone book.

Vision Equipment/Devices

1. **Portable magnifiers**—Some devices can be placed directly on the reading material to allow the user to adjust the magnification without moving the device away from that material. Other devices can be used on a desktop computer and are compatible with magnification software and Windows operating systems. There are also pocket-size devices available for sight-impaired people who are traveling but which can also be used at home.

2. **LCD CCTV magnifier**—A flexible device for seeing at any distance by pointing the camera at what you want to see. It can also be used like a mirror for personal grooming or for magnifying items that are farther away. CCTV magnifiers are available with a 19-, 22- or 24-inch screen.

3. **Rotating Camera**—A computer-compatible device that enables the user to perform daily tasks by rotating a camera for reading, writing, grooming, and magnifying images at any distance.

4. **Desktop video magnifier with text-to-speech capability**—This device will read aloud any printed text.

Organizations that offer services for the visually impaired include: the Lions Club Sight Services at www.lionsclub. org or 630-571-5466 (headquarters); the World Services for the Blind at www.lwsb.org or 800-248-0734. These services provide training in techniques that can help the impaired person function independently in daily living situations, suggestions on available state-of-the-art electronic and optical devices, and instruction on how to use them.

Hearing Equipment/Devices

1. **Hearing aids**—These are the most common devices to address hearing loss, and they range from very tiny ones that fit completely in the ear canal to larger ones that are placed behind a person's ear. Hearing aids will not correct hearing loss but they will help seniors hear better in many circumstances. Modern hearing aids are now digital, permitting more precise corrections to the pattern of specific hearing losses in addition to other features. While it is best to wear a hearing aid in each ear, a person's hearing requirements or economic considerations may dictate the use of only a single hearing aid.

2. **Telecoil**—A telecoil is a device that can be included in a hearing aid to enable a person to use hearing-aid-compatible phones and other technology. The telecoil transforms the hearing aid into a wireless receiver.

3. **Cochlear implant**—These implants are used by people with severe and profound hearing loss, commonly referred to as sensorineural hearing loss or nerve deafness, although most

sensorineural loss is a result of damage to the inner ear (cochlea) rather than to the hearing nerve.

4. **Other implants**—Some types of conductive hearing losses can be surgically corrected with implants such as a bone-conduction hearing device or an osseointegrated device, both of which involve anchoring the device to bone to affect sound vibrations. Conductive hearing loss occurs when sound is not conducted efficiently through the outer ear canal to the eardrum and to the tiny bones of the middle ear.

5. **Assistive Listening Devices (ALDs)**—When a hearing aid or implant is not sufficient, ALDs help separate those sounds a person wants to hear from general background noise. These devices consist of a microphone to collect sound, a transmitter to send the signal across a distance, a receiver to intercept the signal, and any one of several different listening attachments to get the sound from the receiver.

6. **Telephones (landline and cell phones)**—The Federal Communications Commission (FCC) has established rules for both types of phones in order to ensure compatibility with hearing devices. For regulation information, visit the website at www.fcc.gov or call 888-225-5322. To purchase an appropriate wireless product and service, contact CTIA-The Wireless Association at www.accesswireless.org or call 202-736-3200. Consult with your local landline carrier regarding hearing impaired services.

7. **Telephone (captioned)**—This phone allows a hearing-impaired user to read a display while

listening to the caller. It is similar to captioned television. Some states offer special programs or reduced rates. To find out what your state offers, visit CAPTEL at www.captel.com or call 888-269-7477.

For support with hearing loss and to research available technologies, visit the website of Hearing Loss of America at www.hearingloss.org or call 301-657-2248. That website can also direct you to local chapters in your area.

Physical Mobility Equipment/Devices

1. **Walkers and rollators**—Forget old-time, clunky aluminum walkers. In order to make those walkers more user friendly, tennis balls have to be attached to the legs for smoother mobility. Yes, those are still available but why not upgrade (if economically feasible) to the Cadillac of walkers, referred to as "walkers/rollators." There are several models from which to choose. They come in shiny colors and are equipped with wheels, seats, baskets, backrests, footrests, and brakes. This type of equipment makes it much easier for seniors to navigate and offers more stability. Also available is the three-wheel rollator, designed with a frame that allows it to be folded for easy storage and transport, as well as providing better maneuverability through narrow passageways.

2. **Walking canes**—Many seniors do not relish the thought of being seen using a walker, as it broadcasts their deteriorating physical health. Though a cane does not offer the stability of a walker, it can be a

good place to start if a senior needs support but is embarrassed to use a walker. A "sure-footed" cane, which offers better stability than most, is the quad cane with four "feet" attached to the bottom. There are also canes that fold out to make a seat available. Some canes have lighting for safety at night; and some canes fold up for ease in packing or carrying.

3. **Wheelchairs**—New innovations in recent years have created more user friendly wheelchairs. For example, there are wheelchairs that weigh less than nineteen pounds, making them very portable, much easier to fold and much easier to lift into a vehicle. Some have the ability to recline, while others can be used in a shower or for toilet use. There are also battery-operated models that can move under their own power.

4. **Lift recliner chair**—This chair has controls that allow the user to adjust the height and positions of the seat and the chair. These adjustments include: (1) lifting the user from a seated to a standing position, (2) lowering the user from an accessible seated position, and (3) reclining the back into a "sleeper" position. Many of my clients have found this type of recliner so comfortable that they prefer to sleep in one rather than in a bed.

5. **Toilet seat riser**—The riser fits on the toilet seat to add height to the seating area, allowing for ease of getting on and off the toilet. This is especially helpful for people who have knee problems or have lost muscle tone in their legs. Risers also come with arms to permit the user to push up from the seat,

thus increasing stability (the arms are removable). If comfort is important, padded seats are also available.

6. **Walk-in Bath/Whirlpool**—The bathtub that your parent loved to soak in after a difficult day of work and childrearing could now be considered a menace due to his or her limited mobility. If your parent still enjoys the relaxing effects of a bath, or even whirlpool, a walk-in tub might be a good investment. There are many different models to choose from, with features such as leg massage and wheelchair accessibility.

7. **Electric mobility scooter**—This powered device is similar to a golf cart. Typically, scooters have three wheels but four-wheel models are also available. Electric scooters help those with marginal walking capability to conserve energy and travel longer distances within their community. Users should have good sitting balance, enough strength to transfer themselves to and from the scooter, and at least one arm that is strong enough to steer. When selecting a scooter, consider whether it will be used indoors only, outdoors only, or both. Four-wheel scooters are usually more stable but less portable. Be sure to check with the local police department concerning regulations pertaining to the use of the scooter on city streets. Ensure that the scooter is an appropriate size and weight for the individual and that complete training is received prior to use. *Note:* One of my clients had a motorized scooter and, unfortunately, she turned on the ignition before she was seated. The scooter took off without her, causing her considerable injury.

8. **Electric tricycle**—A trike (three wheels) may be a better option for many seniors because it's easier to handle than an electric scooter. There is a pedal assist feature that automatically kicks in as the user pedals, making the bike glide with minimal effort. A throttle on the handlebar allows riding along with or without pedaling. Some models have a reverse option for backing up to park or to maneuver around obstacles. If the tricyclist plans to use the device to go to the grocery store, a metal basket is included for carrying cargo.

9. **Stairway lift**—Stairs are the bane of an elderly person's existence. When people are young and agile, they do not give a second thought to having a home with a staircase. As they age, many people have the foresight to move into a single-level house. However, some find it difficult to give up a home in which they have lived for most of their adult lives, a place that holds many of their most cherished memories. In this case, changes can be made to make even a two-story house more senior friendly. For example, rooms on the lower level of a home can be renovated into a bedroom and bathroom. If this is not possible, a stairway lift is a good and perhaps necessary option. The lift consists of a cushioned chair, arm rests, and a foot rest, all of which can be folded up. It is battery operated and the lift's chair is propelled either up or down the staircase on a special railing that is attached to

a wall or to an existing banister. These lifts can be used on curved, straight, or outdoor staircases.

Monitoring Equipment/Devices

I cannot stress enough the importance of medical alert/monitoring systems for those individuals who live alone or reside in large facilities. Throughout the years, many of my clients have fallen in their homes and yards. Some of them did not have a monitoring system and could not reach a phone to call for help. They suffered severe injuries and some nearly died after lying for hours or days on the floor or ground until someone found them. The installation cost and monthly fees for a monitoring system are a very small price to pay considering the possible devastating consequences of not having this safety feature.

1. **Pendant or wrist medical alert**—This is the most common form of alert device. It is worn as a pendant around the neck or like a watch on the wrist. The user pushes a button that summons help in the form of a neighbor, family member or ambulance, depending on the situation. Many of these devices are waterproof so that they can be worn in the bath or shower. Some companies offer an alert device that can automatically place a call for help if the device detects a fall and the wearer is unable to push the button.

2. **GPS tracking**—When activated, this mobile device pinpoints the subscriber's location using satellites. The operator can communicate with the subscriber over the speaker on the device and dispatch the necessary assistance. This is a wonderful piece of technology for those on-the-go seniors. Tracking

devices are also available to locate seniors suffering from memory problems, such as Alzheimer's.

3. **Baby monitor**—If your parent lives at home with a caregiver in attendance, consider purchasing baby monitors that can be placed in different areas of the home, such as in bathrooms or bedrooms. These monitors are offered with audio, video, and movement features and are helpful in alerting the caregiver in the event a situation occurs that requires immediate assistance.

4. **Home alarm systems**—To protect the safety and security of your parent in his or her residence, home alarm systems should be installed. Some also feature medical alert capability and can be connected to local police, ambulance, and fire stations.

CHAPTER 23

YOUR PERSONAL SUPPORT GROUP

"All would live long, but none would be old." —Ben Franklin

When you start managing your parent's affairs, at whatever level, it is helpful for you to have a support group to balance your life and to help keep your sanity. This group will possibly include family members and friends who can provide emotional support and even some caretaking responsibility. However, the expertise and information that you may require will most likely need to come from outside sources.

Throughout this book, I have noted many resources to assist you on various issues. You may discover that, in some cases, these can be used as stepping stones to other resources that can provide in-depth information on narrow topics. Not all agencies will be able to provide information appropriate to your parent's situation, but they can supply names of other agencies that may be more helpful.

The resources listed below summarize and expand upon the resources noted in the previous chapters. They have been divided up into different categories, with some resources appearing in more than one category. *Please note that contact information may have changed since this book's publication.*

LISTING OF RESOURCES REFERENCED IN THE BOOK'S TEXT

Local Resources

Since city, county, and state resources differ from area to area, specifics for your location cannot be detailed. Noted below are general resources, as well as some that can point you to information specific to your locality. If all else fails, you can access Internet websites or pick up a phone book and search under "government" and "senior services" listings.

- *Adult Day Care*: These centers enable seniors to socialize, while still receiving needed care services, and can offer caregivers a respite from caregiving responsibilities. Contact county social services, the health department, mental health centers, a local senior center, or your family physician. You can also contact the Administration for Community Living at www.acl.gov or call 202-619-0724, or visit the website of Help Guide at www.helpguide.com.

- *County Social Service Agencies*: Social service agencies provide an array of services geared to seniors, ranging from assistance with Medicare and Medicaid to housing and caregiving information. One of the most important departments within these agencies is Adult Protective Services (APS), whose function is to assess living conditions of those seniors considered "at risk" and to investigate elder abuse. While these agencies may go by different names, you should be able to locate the one in your particular county by accessing the government pages in your telephone book, by doing an Internet search, or by contacting social workers or physicians.

- *Estate Attorney or Elder Law Attorney*: An estate attorney provides expertise in legal matters relating to wills, trusts, Medicaid, conservatorships, and various legal issues that affect the elderly. For referrals and more information, contact the National Academy of Elder Law Attorneys at www.naela.org or call 703-942-5711. You can also contact your state's Bar Association (a professional body of lawyers).

- *Hospitals*: Many hospitals have social service departments, with some especially geared toward seniors.

- *Law Enforcement*: Contact your local police department if you suspect illegal activity directed toward your parent such as physical or financial abuse.

- *Meals on Wheels*: Contact your local senior center or county social service agency for information, or visit the website of the Meals on Wheels Association of America at www.mowaa.org.

- *Physicians*: Besides a good "bedside manner," it is important that your parent has a doctor who is well versed in geriatric medicine. Your local hospital should be able to provide you with referrals. Also, you can access the Internet to find a doctor

who is a geriatric specialist or you can visit the
website of the Federation of State Medical Boards
at www.fsmb.org, or call them at 817-868-4000.

- *Religious Establishments*: Many churches,
  synagogues, and other religious entities offer
  services for seniors who are in their congregation.

- *Senior Centers*: As mentioned in this book,
  these centers not only offer social activities for
  the active senior but also provide references
  to agencies and programs that can assist your
  senior with problems or concerns. Contact your
  city hall to find the location of a center near
  your parent's residence. If the city hall cannot
  provide this information, your county's social
  services department will be able to do so.

- *Social Workers (private)*: Your county social service
  agency is staffed with social workers who can assist
  seniors with many issues. However, their caseload is
  tremendous and the number of social workers has been
  cut due to budgetary constraints. Private social workers
  are an alternative if your parent is experiencing a
  problem that needs immediate attention. These social
  workers can devote more time to addressing problems
  and are often able to achieve faster results. They do not
  come cheap, but in the long run, they could save you
  and your parent a great deal of headache, heartache,
  and possibly money. The key is to look for a social
  worker who has experience in geriatric care. Geriatric
  care managers (social workers) can navigate through

the maze of government bureaucracies, find medical specialists, and provide caregiver referrals, to name just a few of their abilities. Your county social service agency may be able to provide you with referrals or you can visit the following websites: (1) National Association of Social Workers at www.socialworkers.org or call 202-408-8600 or (2) National Association of Professional Geriatric Care Managers at www.caremanager.org or call 520-881-8008.

- *State Attorney General's Office*: The contact information for your state attorney general's office can be found in the telephone book under the "government" section or at www.naag.org. If you have any legal questions or concerns, this office should be able to either help you directly or refer you to the appropriate agency.

- *State Health Department*: For your state's health department contact information, check listings under the "government" section of the phone book, visit www.medicare.gov/contacts or call 800-633-4227.

CAREGIVING

- *Administration for Community Living* at www.acl.gov or call 206-619-0724

- *Family Caregiver Alliance/National Center on Caregiving* at www.caregiver.org or call 800-445-8106

- *County social services, geriatric care managers* (private social workers)

FINANCIAL RESOURCES

- *Certified Public Account (CPA)*: Your parent may already have a CPA and, if so, that person will be a valuable resource for advice on tax-related matters and the preparation of tax returns. If you need to find a CPA, consult with relatives and friends for recommendations or check with your state's licensing board. CPAs are only one of three tax professionals (the other two being tax attorneys and enrolled agents) who can interact with the Internal Revenue Service (IRS) on a client's behalf. Since tax laws are very complex, spending extra money for the advice and assistance of a CPA could actually save considerably more money down the road.

- *Consumer Financial Protection Bureau*: To file a complaint about a financial product, a credit card company, or a credit reporting agency, call 855-411-2372 or visit their website at www.consumerfinance.gov.

- *Credit Reporting Agencies*: To request credit reports, visit the website of annualcreditreport. com or call Equifax at 800-685-1111, Experian at 888-397-3742 or TransUnion at 800-916-8800.

- *Federal Trade Commission (FTC)*: For information on identity theft, visit the FTC website at www. ftc.gov/idtheft. For reporting identity theft, visit the FTC complaint website at www. ftccomplaintassistant.gov or call 877-438-4338.

- *Fiduciary*: A public or private fiduciary manages money and property. To find one in your state, contact your local county social services, an elder law attorney, or go online.

- *Financial Advisor (Independent)*: A financial advisor offers advice on financial planning and investment products. Ensure your advisor is truly independent and is a Registered Investment Advisor (RIA) or an Investment Advisor Representative (IAR) who works for an RIA. Only RIAs/IARs are legally required to act in the best interest of their client. To check on the background of an advisor, call the Financial Industry Regulatory Authority (FINRA) at 301-590-6500 or visit their website at www.finra.org.

- *Office of Comptroller of the Currency*: This agency regulates all national banks and federal savings associations. If you are experiencing a problem with a bank account or with a bank-issued credit card, call 800-613-6743 or visit their website at www.occ.treas.gov.

- *State Controller's Office/Treasury Office*: For information on reclaiming unclaimed property.

GENERAL

- *Administration for Community Living* at www.acl.gov or call 202-619-0724

- *American Association of Retired Persons (AARP)* at www.aarp.org or call 888-687-2277

- *American Seniors Association (ASA)* at www.americanseniors.org or call 800-951-0017

- *CAPTEL—Captioned Telephones* at www.captel.com or call 888-269-7477

- *Centers for Disease Control and Prevention* at www.cdc.gov or call 800-232-4636

- *Charity Navigator* at www.charitynavigator.org

- *CTIA-The Wireless Association* at www.accesswireless.org or call 202-736-3200

- *Federal Communications Commission (FCC)* at www.fcc.gov or call 888-225-5322

- *Help Guide* at www.helpguide.org for issues affecting the aging population

- *Internal Revenue Service* at www.irs.gov (or call your local IRS office; look in the phone book or visit the website for local office information)

- *Meals on Wheels Association of America* at www.mowaa.org or call county social services or a local senior center

HEALTHCARE PROVIDERS

- *Federation of State Medical Boards* at www.fsmb.org or call 817-868-4000

- *Hospice Association of America* at www.nahc.org/haa or 202-546-4759

- *Hospice Foundation of America* at www.hospicefoundation.org or 800-854-3402

- *National Hospice & Palliative Care Organization* at www.nhpco.org or 800-658-8898

LEGAL RESOURCES

- *Estate or Elder Law Attorney*: contact your state's Bar Association or the National Academy of Elder Law Attorneys at www.naela.org, or call 703-942-5711

- *Fiduciary (Private or Public)*: search on-line for a fiduciary in your state; contact county social services or an elder law attorney

- *Local Law Enforcement*

- *State Attorney General's Office* at www.naag.org

MEDICAL INSURANCE

- *Long-Term Care*:
- American Association for Long-Term Care Insurance at www.aaltci.org or call 818-597-3227
- Medicare at www.medicare.gov/ltcplanning or call 800-633-4227
- National Association of Insurance Commissioners at 866-470-6242
- U.S. Dept. of Health and Human Services at www.longtermcare.gov or call 202-619-0724

- Independent financial advisor, estate or elder law attorney, or county social services

- *Medicaid* at www.medicaid.gov, or your state's Medicaid office, or an elder law attorney

- *Medicare* at www.medicare.gov or 800-633-4227

- *Social Services* at local levels

- *State Health Department* at www.medicare.gov/contacts or 800-633-4227

- *Tricare*—healthcare coverage for active or retired military personnel at www.tricare.mil or call: North Region at 866-307-9749; South Region at 800-554-2397; West Region at 800-558-1746

- *Veterans Administration* at www.va.gov or 800-827-1000

MENTAL HEALTH

- *Alzheimer's Association* at www.alz.org or 800-272-3900

- *Alzheimer's Foundation of America* at www.alzfdn.org or 866-232-8484

- *Alzheimer's Disease Education & Referral Center of the National Institute on Aging* at www.nia.nih.gov/alzheimers or 800-438-4380

- *Centers for Disease Control and Prevention* at www.cdc.gov or call 800-232-4636

- *National Institute of Neurological Disorders & Stroke* at www.ninds.nih.gov or 800-352-9424

- *National Institute on Drug Abuse* at www.drugabuse.gov or 301-443-1124

- *Seniors in Sobriety* at www.seniorsinsobriety.org.

- *Substance Abuse and Mental Health Services Administration* at www.hhs.gov or call 240-276-2000

PHYSICAL HEALTH

- *Agency for Healthcare Research and Quality* at www.ahrq.gov or call 301-427-1364

- *Centers for Disease Control and Prevention* at www.cdc.gov or call 800-232-4636

- *Federation of State Medical Boards* at www.fsmb.org

- *Hearing Loss Association of America* at www.hearingloss.org or 301-657-2248

- *Hospice Association of America* at www.nahc.org/haa or 202-546-4759

- *Hospice Foundation of America* at www.hospicefoundation.org or 800-854-3402

- *Lions Clubs Sight Services* at www.lionsclubs.org or 630-571-5466

- *Meals on Wheels Association of America* at www.mowaa.org

- *National Hospice & Palliative Care Organization* at www.nhpco.org or 800-658-8898

- *National Institute of Neurological Disorders & Stroke* at www.ninds.nih.gov or 800-352-9424

- *National Institute on Drug Abuse* at www.drugabuse.gov or 301-443-1124

- *Seniors in Sobriety* at www.seniorsinsobriety.org

- *Substance Abuse and Mental Health Services Administration* at www.hhs.gov or call 240-276-2000

- *World Services for the Blind* at www.lwsb.org or call 800-248-0734

RETIREMENT

- *Social Security* at www.ssa.gov or 800-772-1213

- *Financial Advisor (Independent)*: A financial advisor offers advice on retirement planning and investment products.

SOCIAL WORKERS (GERIATRIC CARE MANAGERS)

- *National Association of Professional Geriatric Care Managers* at www.caremanager.org or 520-881-8008

- *National Association of Social Workers* at www.socialworkers.org or 202-408-8600

CHAPTER 24
WORDS TO LIVE BY??
(OLD-AGE ADAGES)

QUOTATIONS ABOUT GROWING OLD, FROM PHYLLIS DILLER TO BENJAMIN FRANKLIN

If you live long enough the venerability factor creeps in; you get accused of things you never did and praised for virtues you never had.

—I. F. Stone

All would live long, but none would be old.

—Ben Franklin

Growing old is like being increasingly penalized for a crime you have not committed.

—Anthony Powell

If I'd known I was gonna live this long [100 years], I'd have taken better care of myself.

—James Hubert Blake

To keep the heart unwrinkled, to be hopeful, kindly, cheerful, reverent - that is to triumph over old age.

—Thomas Bailey Aldrich

Growing old is no more than a bad habit which a busy man has no time to form.

—Andri Maurois

Age is a high price to pay for maturity.

—Tom Stoppard

I'm very pleased with each advancing year. It stems back to when I was forty. I was a bit upset about reaching that milestone, but an older friend consoled me. "Don't complain about growing old—many people don't have that privilege."

—Earl Warren

Middle age is when you have a choice of two temptations and choose the one that will get you home earlier.

—Unknown

Growing old—it's not nice, but it's interesting.

—August Strindberg

They tell you that you'll lose your mind when you grow older. What they don't tell you is that you won't miss it very much.

—Malcolm Cowley

Age is a question of mind over matter. If you don't mind, it doesn't matter.

—Leroy "Satchel" Paige

Do not regret growing older. It is a privilege denied to many.
                                                          —Unknown

I still have a full deck; I just shuffle slower now.
                                                          —Unknown

We've put more effort into helping folks reach old age than into helping them enjoy it.
                                                          —Frank A. Clark

Everything slows down with age, except the time it takes cake and ice cream to reach your hips.
                                                 —Attributed to John Wagner

Old age ain't no place for sissies.
                                                          —Bette Davis

Wrinkled was not one of the things I wanted to be when I grew up.
                                                          —Unknown

Don't let aging get you down. It's too hard to get back up.
                                                 —Attributed to John Wagner

You spend 90% of your adult life hoping for a long rest and the last 10% trying to convince the Lord that you're actually not that tired.
                                                          —Robert Brault

You know you're getting old when all the names in your black book have M.D. after them.
                                                          —Arnold Palmer

The elderly don't drive that badly; they're just the only ones with time to do the speed limit.

—Jason Love

That [senior citizen] driver has nowhere to go and all day to get there!

—Bruce Harrison

Old age puts more wrinkles in our minds than on our faces.

—Michel de Montaigne

Regular naps prevent old age, especially if you take them while driving.

—Unknown

I don't know how you feel about old age...but in my case I didn't even see it coming. It hit me from the rear.

—Phyllis Diller

All diseases run into one, old age.

—Ralph Waldo Emerson

SUMMARY

Definition of denial: a refusal to recognize or acknowledge.

Denial is the most common problem I have encountered when working with seniors and their families. Denial leads to a mind-set that can cause crises involving both financial and physical health. The main reason I wrote this book is to help caretakers and seniors overcome this mind-set.

There are many excuses for denial, some of which include:

- *Fear of the unknown*—"I don't know where to turn or what to expect."

- *Hectic personal and work life*—"I don't have the time or the energy to deal with the issues my parent is facing."

- *Fear of death*—"I can't face my parent's mortality—or my own."

After reading this book, you *do* know what to expect and where to turn. I have provided you with a primer that addresses the major issues facing seniors and their families and have referred you to a multitude of resources.

Yes, you will feel overwhelmed with the prospect of not only raising a family and working but also caring for your parent. However, you now have a guide to help you anticipate the situations that arise with aging. The earlier you start to prepare yourself, the more time you will have to plan for the situations you may be called upon to handle. By researching resources and getting those resources in place beforehand, you will save yourself an enormous amount of time and aggravation.

Your unresolved feelings about death will not delay the inevitable. If needed, seek the counsel of a mental health professional or find someone to step in as your parent's primary caretaker. Do not let your parent struggle alone through his or her end-of-life issues.

Procrastination and paralysis, fueled by denial, will only lead to problems that will become more difficult to resolve. Your parent's physical, emotional and financial well-being could be placed in jeopardy. So "bite the bullet" and get moving. And remember, you are not alone! For over fifteen years, I have been consulting with seniors and their families regarding aging issues. If you hit the proverbial brick wall, contact me at my website, as noted below.

Wendy Harrison
Have Pen Will Travel, LLC
Consulting Services for Seniors
www.assistyoursenior.com

APPENDIX

CAREGIVER TIMESHEET SAMPLE

Hourly Wage: $_____
Mileage Rate: $_____cents/mile

SERVICE DATE	CAREGIVER NAME	TIME IN	TIME OUT	MILES DRIVEN

TOTAL HOURS	WAGES & MILEAGE DUE	AMOUNT OF REIMB. EXPENSES*	TOTAL AMOUNT PAID	DATE PAID
	$	$	$	

* Submit Receipt(s)

PETTY CASH ACCOUNT LOG SAMPLE

DATE OF EXPENSE	AMOUNT OF EXPENSE	REASON OR STORE	DEPOSIT TO PETTY CASH	DEPOSIT DATE	PETTY CASH BALANCE
	$		$		$

1. Unless your parent has a lot of expenses that can only be paid by cash, the most that should be kept in petty cash is $300.00.

2. Using a box that can be locked with a key is the best way to store the petty cash. Keep the box and key out of sight so that only you and the caregiver know their location. The key should not be hidden with the box but in a separate place.

3. When setting up petty cash, keep the log in a file folder next to the box so that the caregiver can write in the information as the cash is used. For the initial deposit of cash, note on the log the amount deposited into the account under "deposit to petty cash" and the balance under "petty cash balance."

4. The caregiver should keep all receipts for purchases and place them in the petty cash box or attach them to the log.

5. The petty cash should be balanced at least every two weeks and money added as necessary.

MEDICAL BILLING
RECONCILIATION FORM SAMPLE

MEDICAL PROVIDER: _____

PATIENT: _____

SERVICE DATE	AMOUNT BILLED	MEDICARE WRITEOFF	MEDICARE PAYMENT	DATE PAID

SECONDARY INSURANCE PAYMENT	DATE PAID	COMMENTS	PATIENT PAYMENT AMOUNT	DATE PAID

GUIDELINES FOR SETTING UP A FILING SYSTEM

Here are the tools you need to set up an easy-to-use filing system:

1. a filing cabinet (two-drawer style should be sufficient) or plastic file box(s); whichever one is chosen should have "runners" or "tracks" on which to slide hanging file folders

2. hanging file folders with plastic tabs and inserts

3. file folders—one-third cut (this designates the position of the tab on the file folder)

4. file folder labels

5. file boxes with lids to store older files

To set up files in a filing cabinet, you should create main headings or sections with which to label the hanging file folders. For example, a main heading could be "Banking" or "Insurance." Take the paper tab that comes in the box of the hanging file folders, write the name of the main heading on it and insert in the plastic tab. Position the plastic tab on the hanging file folder and place the folder in the file cabinet.

The one-third cut file folders are used to designate subheadings or topics within the main heading. For example, under the main heading of "Banking," you might place a folder labeled "Bank of America Checking Account Statements—2014."

The following outline provides a model for the sections in a file system. Main headings should be alphabetized and the subheadings alphabetized within the main heading.

MODEL OF THE SECTIONS IN A FILING SYSTEM

AUTOMOBILE
  DMV Records (use separate file for each auto)
  Maintenance & Repairs (use separate file for each auto)

BANKING
  Checking Account Statements (file by bank name and year)
  Safe Deposit Box
  Savings Account Statements (file by bank name and year)

CREDIT CARDS
  Mastercard
  VISA

HOME MAINTENANCE
  Housekeeping
  Landscaping
  Pool Service
  Repairs

INCOME TAXES
  Tax Return—2014
  Tax Return—2013

IN-HOME SERVICES
  Caregiving Agency

INSURANCE
  Automobile
  Home
  Life
  Long-Term Care
  Medical

MODEL OF THE SECTIONS IN A FILING SYSTEM (CONT'D.)

INVESTMENTS
Brokerage Accounts
Stocks

LEGAL
Trust
Will

LOANS
Automobile
Home Mortgage

MEDICAL EQUIPMENT
Oxygen Rental
Wheelchair Purchase

MEDICAL INSURANCE PAYMENTS
Medicare Statements
Supplemental Insurance Statements

MEDICAL SERVICE PROVIDERS
Dentist
Doctor(s)

MEMBERSHIPS
Clubs
Organizations

PHARMACY
Drug Receipts

MODEL OF THE SECTIONS IN A FILING SYSTEM (CONT'D.)

PROPERTY (documents pertaining to the purchase and/or sale of property)

PROPERTY TAX
   Home
   Vacation Home

RETIREMENT
   Pension
   Social Security

SUBSCRIPTIONS
   Magazines
   Newspapers

TRAVEL
   Airline information

UTILITIES
   Electric & Gas
   Sanitary Service
   Telephone
   Water

WARRANTIES
   Appliances
   Furniture

RECOMMENDED RECORDS RETENTION GUIDELINES

TYPE OF RECORD	RETENTION PERIOD*
Automobile (DMV, Maintenance)	Until automobile is sold
Bank Receipts (Deposit and Withdrawal Slips, ATM slips)	Until bank statement is received and reconciled
Bank Statements	7 years
Checks—Cancelled (For Important Payments)	Permanently
Contracts (Mortgage Loans)	7 years if expired; permanently if still in effect
Correspondence (Legal; Important Matters)	Permanently
Correspondence (General)	2 years
Credit Card Receipts	Until credit card statement is received and reconciled, or keep for warranty/tax records
Credit Card Statements	1 year; 7 years if any charges are used for deductions on tax returns
Deeds	7 years after the sale
Financial Documents - Stocks/Bonds - Brokerage Statements	 - 7 years beyond selling - 7 years
Home Repair Bills & Contracts - Major Work - Minor Work	 - 10 years - 2 years or as long as work is under warranty
Insurance Policies	Life of the policy
Insurance Claims	6 years
Medical Records	7 years if fees are claimed on tax return; 5 years generally
Medical Insurance Payments	See "Medical Records," above

---

*   This retention information is provided only as a guideline. Consult your CPA or attorney before disposing of any significant financial or legal paperwork.

Mortgage Statements	Term of ownership plus 7 years
Personal Health Records (Physician Contact Info, Medical History, Medication List)	Permanently
Receipts—General	Unless needed for tax return or warranty, discard "cash" receipts immediately and "credit card" receipts after credit card statement has been reconciled
Retirement/Pension Records	Permanently
Tax Return & Back-up Documentation	7 years
Utility Bills	1 year unless needed for tax return
Warranty Documents	Until warranty expires (keep sales receipts with the warranty information)

ARE YOU SAVVY ABOUT SENIOR ISSUES?

Test yourself on senior topics and issues. Answers appear at the end of the questionnaire.

1. Medicare automatically provides healthcare benefits for all Americans once they reach the age of 65. True or False or I don't know?
2. The most common form of elder abuse is neglect. True or False or I don't know?
3. Long-term care insurance pays for prescribed medications. True or False or I don't know?
4. The age at which you receive full Social Security benefits depends on your year of birth. True or False or I don't know?
5. When hiring a non-agency caregiver, the Internal Revenue Service may consider the caregiver an employee and you will be required to report their earnings and withhold taxes. True or False or I don't know?
6. The "donut hole" in Medicare Part D refers to an option whereby the insured does not have to pay for over-the-counter medication. True or False or I don't know?
7. A divorced spouse is eligible for Social Security benefits based on their ex's allowance if the marriage lasted 10 years or more. True or False or I don't know?
8. Medicaid automatically provides healthcare coverage for all Americans once they reach the age of 65. True or False or I don't know?

9. Board and care facilities offer more caregiving services than senior apartments. True or False or I don't know?

10. The provisions of "The Patient Protection and Affordable Care of Act of 2010" only affect healthcare coverage for those under age 65. True or False or I don't know?

11. If you die without a will or trust, state law controls and distributes property and assets. True or False or I don't know?

12. A medical alarm or monitoring device is not necessary if a senior has a cell phone. True or False or I don't know?

13. It is wise to pay medical bills upon receipt, regardless if the insurance companies have issued payments. True or False or I don't know?

14. Medicare does not cover hospice care unless the patient is destitute. True or False or I don't know?

15. People confined to wheelchairs benefit from exercise programs. True or False or I don't know?

16. A conservator is appointed by a court to manage the assets of an incapacitated person. True or False or I don't know?

17. Binge drinking is not a significant problem in people over the age of 65. True or False or I don't know?

18. Senior centers and adult day care centers provide housing for those who can no longer live alone. True or False or I don't know?

19. A walker offers more stability than a cane. True or False or I don't know?

20. It is not necessary for single, sexually active seniors to be tested for STDs. True or False or I don't know?
21. Medicare will pay for long-term care in an assisted living facility. True or False or I don't know?
22. A geriatric doctor specializes in the healthcare problems of elderly patients. True or False or I don't know?
23. Alzheimer's disease is not the most common form of dementia. True or False or I don't know?
24. The aging process begins in the womb. True or False or I don't know?

<u>Answers:</u>

1.	False	13.	False
2.	True	14.	False
3.	False	15.	True
4.	True	16.	True
5.	True	17.	False
6.	False	18.	False
7.	True	19.	True
8.	False	20.	False
9.	True	21.	False
10.	False	22.	True
11.	True	23.	False
12.	False	24.	True

<u>Scoring</u>:

If you correctly answered 22 questions or more, you are well above average in your understanding of senior issues, so this book will be a helpful reference guide.

If you correctly answered 19 to 21 questions, reading this book will enhance your understanding of senior issues.

If you correctly answered 16 to 18 questions, this book will be an important guide to your understanding of senior issues.

If you correctly answered less than 16 questions, this book is essential to your understanding of senior issues. You have no time to waste!

INDEX